DATE DUE

Entering & Succeeding in Emerging Countries

marketing to the forgotten majority

A. Coskun Samli

University of North Florida

THOMSON

™

SOUTH-WESTERN

Australia · Canada · Mexico · Singapore · Spain · United Kingdom · United States

THOMSON

———✳———™

SOUTH-WESTERN

Entering and Succeeding in Emerging Countries: Marketing to the Forgotten Majority

A. Coskin Samli

VP/Editorial Director:
Jack W. Calhoun

VP/Editor-in-Chief:
Dave Shaut

Acquisitions Editor:
Steve Momper

Editorial Counselor:
Michael R. Czinkota

Production Editor:
Darrell E. Frye

Production Manager:
Patricia Matthews Boies

Manufacturing Coordinator:
Charlene Taylor

Senior Design Project Manager:
Michelle Kunkler

Cover Designer:
R. Alcom

Cover Image:
PhotoDisc, Inc.

Production House:
Argosy

Printer:
Phoenix Book Technology
Hagerstown, MD

For permission to use material from this text or product, contact us by
Tel (800) 730-2214
Fax (800) 730-2215
http://www.thomsonrights.com

For more information
contact South-Western,
5191 Natorp Boulevard,
Mason, Ohio, 45040.
Or you can visit our Internet site at: http://www.swlearning.com

TABLE of Contents

"This book is dedicated to international entrepreneurs every-where. May they become instrumental in developing a better world as they profit from their toil."

PREFACE

This book is written on the basis of five key premises. The first one is that global giants are entering the rich markets from the higher end and staying exclusively in these markets. Hence, they are forgetting the majority of people in the world. This concept is called corporate imperialism.

The second premise is that the forgotten majority has needs and substantial, although limited, income. The needs of these markets are not being satisfied, and they must be taken care of.

The third premise is that scattered and varied niche markets of the world create the forgotten majority. This market is very large and likely to grow faster than the industrialized markets of the world.

The fourth premise is that global giants lack the capability and flexibility required to cater to the forgotten majority. In addition, if these companies do consider the majority of the world's population, they are not able to do a good job of meeting consumers' needs.

The fifth and final premise is that small- and medium-size entrepreneurial companies can perform well in markets where the forgotten majority resides. These firms are flexible, are close to the market, have a better understanding of consumer needs, and are capable of partnering with local firms to do the job. As small- and medium-size companies deliver consumer value and create consumer satisfaction, they also are likely to profit financially, which is the reward for their willingness to take care of the unsatisfied need of the forgotten majority. Whereas global giants cannot make enough money catering to the forgotten majority, small entrepreneurial Western companies can engage in profitable ventures in the markets where the forgotten majority resides. Major profit opportunities in the world markets are located in the third world. All five premises mentioned point to potential lucrative business opportunities—not for all businesses, just those that are small and efficient.

This book discusses the need for a second wave of globalization. Companies must cater to the second, third, or fourth tiers of world markets, entering the markets from low-end mass marketing so most of the forgotten majority can be taken care of. By satisfying the needs of the forgotten majority, companies can reverse the current trend of widening the gap between the haves and have-nots. Indeed, only then will it be possible to experience a sustainable globalization activity that benefits the whole world, not only the rich and privileged. Accomplishing this end, particularly by engagement in profitable partnerships and trading blocs, is promising and desirable.

This book reinforces the belief that catering to the forgotten majority is not only an important activity, but also a profitable one. Indeed, in a decade or so, the forgotten majority will start asserting itself so it does not remain forgotten. If small proactive entrepreneurial firms start now, they can have an advantage. They are likely to make more money than the latecomers.

So far, only a few attempts have been made to take advantage of the huge and fast-growing third-world market. Small firms can cope with the variety of needs and culture-driven behavior patterns that prevail in these markets. The global giants that thrive on large volumes and economies of scales cannot cater to the variety of needs and behavior patterns.

Many ideas are presented throughout this book. Many of them stem from my travels, research, consulting and teaching international marketing at the undergraduate and graduate levels.

Many people have been helpful in developing this book. If my friend Michael Czinkota of Georgetown University had not encouraged me, this book would not have happened. Steve Momper of Thomson Publishing was encouraging throughout the duration of this project. My dean at the University of North Florida College of Business, Earle Traynham, was always encouraging. My department head, Jay Coleman, was patient in listening to my points of view and responding wisely. My assistant, Juraj Ciz, a young talent from Slovakia, who is now making his mark in the world of international advertising, was helpful in developing estimates and locating references. My brother, Osman Samli, who resides in Turkey, patiently listened to my ideas, did research for me and interacted very wisely as the telephone conversations. My students listened to my ideas and interacted with me often. Joan DelCogliano keyed the entire manuscript. She was able to read my, at times, illegible handwriting. My current secretary, Carolyn Gavin, was very helpful during the revision process. Beverly Chapman, as usual, gave me competent editorial advice. To all of these people, I am grateful. However, I am solely responsible for the ideas and arguments presented throughout. My hope is that this book will make a difference in improving the quality of life of those people who are the core of the forgotten majority.

INTRODUCTION

You may be surprised know that on Indian TV, the Pillsbury Doughboy presses his palms together, bows in the traditional Indian greeting style, and speaks six languages. The Doughboy is promoting a group of higher-margin products, such as microwavable pizza. But Pillsbury found out that in the tradition-bound Indian market, the company must go back to basics. It started thinking about marketing a product it had abandoned in the U.S. market—just plain old flour. This is what is called "foot-in-the-door policy."

Selling packaged flour in India is almost revolutionary. Indian housewives still buy raw wheat in bulk; clean it by hand; store it in huge metal hampers; and every week carry some to a neighborhood mill, which is called a *chakki*, to have it ground between two stones. Wheat is mostly used to prepare *roti*, a flat bread prepared on a griddle that is used in every meal. Indians traditionally eat with their hands and use roti as a spoon. At this point in time, approximately less than 1 percent of all whole-wheat flour, which is called *atta*, is sold prepackaged. The extremes in climate and poor roads make it difficult to maintain freshness from mill to warehouse, let alone on store shelves.

An Indian housewife must serve the freshest and softest *roti* to her family. The packaged flour is not a moneymaker, but Pillsbury believes in the need to start with that so more profitable products can be introduced in the future. Thus, the company is positioning itself as "a food company."

The introduction of packaged flour means overcoming thousands of years of tradition. In India, the color of food, the aroma, and the feel between the fingers and in the mouth are extremely important. Pillsbury wanted to establish contacts with existing mills, but inspectors found hygiene and safety to be less than desirable. So Pillsbury decided to introduce its packaged wheat through a joint venture. The blue package, which features the Doughboy hoisting a *roti*, has become the market leader in Bombay, India's largest city. Pillsbury promotes the flow of its flour, promising that *rotis* made from it will stay "soft for six hours." There are additives but no artificial preservatives.

This book is about the strategy for entering a new market globally and many similar activities and needs. It is good for both the company and the customer that Pillsbury is trying to establish itself in India, which happens to be a part of the forgotten majority, which will be discussed throughout this book. Pillsbury is a very large company, but unless it achieves a critical sales volume in India, it cannot continue in the Indian market for long. Yet Pillsbury, inevitably, appeals to the first tier of the Indian market in major metropolitan areas. However, more than 700 million Indians are left out of this first tier of the market. Who is going to reach them? In that 700 million plus people who are a big portion of the forgotten majority are some 300 languages and at least as many cultural variations. Certainly the Doughboy will never speak 300 languages. Additionally, there may be many cultural variations regarding the taste of *roti* or other wheat-based products that Pillsbury is planning to market. One size does not fit all, one taste does not appeal to all, and selling products to the well-to-do does not take care of the forgotten majority. Above all, Pillsbury may not be able to make enough money if it doesn't have the necessary sales volume. But small- and medium-size entrepreneurial firms can do very well under these circumstances. Although much need and much opportunity exists for Pillsbury-like activity around the world, international giants shy away from these options. Hence, the forgotten majority in the world gets bigger and becomes less satisfied as consumers. The satisfaction consumers provide to these markets means major profit opportunities.

Consider the following:

- A small bicycle manufacturer from Columbus, Ohio, may wish to enter southeastern Turkey, where public transportation is not plentiful.
- A small pharmaceutical product wholesaler in Jacksonville, Florida, may consider entering a part of Russia where the supply of pharmaceutical products is very limited.
- A medium-size manufacturer of refrigerators from Orlando, Florida, may wish to enter central Africa, where refrigeration is almost nonexistent.

- A medium-size canned food processing firm from Lansing, Michigan, may wish to enter a region of Pakistan where the food supply is inadequate.

The list could go on and on. Perhaps the most critical common thread among these situations is that these markets are not rich. As such, global or multinational giants do not pay attention to them. The important point emphasized throughout this book is that the third-world countries or emerging countries have what has been described as market pyramids. This pyramid is composed of three or four tiers. For instance, it is estimated that only 7 million people in India have an income greater than $20,000, which is tier one. About 63 million people have an income between $10,000 and $20,000, which is tier two. Approximately 125 million Indians make between $5,000 and $10,000, tier three. And over 700 million make less than $5,000 (Prahalad, Lieberthal, and Thurnau 1998). This may be called tier four. Global giants may look at tier one. But what about tiers two, three, and four?

These tiers exist. They have clear-cut needs, and they have some money. They are expecting the imperialist mind-set of multinationals paying attention only to the rich to change so their needs also can be taken care of. Not only do tiers two, three, and four consist of incomparably more people than tier one, but they are also growing faster. Thus, the forgotten majority of the world population is waiting for products and services that will make their lives more palatable. In an international sense, markets are emerging to which not enough attention is being paid. These are the markets where the future action will be.

The elimination of corporate imperialism in India is necessary. It means getting away from high-end rich niche marketing and moving to low-end mass marketing (or specific niche marketing) by appealing to the second, third, and fourth tiers in emerging markets. When 700 million people are making $5,000 or less a year, there is still a tremendous amount of buying power that cannot be ignored. These second, third, and fourth tiers of emerging markets is where the profit potential is now and where even more profit potential exists in the foreseeable future.

As the flow of information facilitates the flow of goods and services throughout the world, it is critical to look at world markets more closely. There are more countries in the world today than ever before, there are more people in the world today than ever before, and there is more information floating around than ever before. All off these factors translate into more needs and demands by consumers and indicate more and more opportunities for international businesses. When more consumers are exposed to an ever-increasing information flow, the opportunities for international business increase more than proportionately. Opportunities increase more than proportionately because those who do not have much income or wealth as consumers have access to information regarding the availability of goods and services and, therefore, have much greater propensity to consume. If the income of these consumers increases marginally, their desire for products and services increases more than proportionately.

Those people who need to consume more because they have not had much are everywhere. They may not have a lot to spend, but they are willing to sacrifice the limited buying power they do have to buy things they have only heard about but never owned. All of these people's buying power translate into potential profits.

Dealing with such markets is not easy. These consumers have limited income; their exact location is not quite known and, in some cases, their needs are not articulated or have not surfaced adequately. Above all, they are scattered all over the world. But despite these and many other barriers and difficulties, international businesses market goods and services to this majority which has, thus far, been neglected. And when these businesses successfully deliver satisfaction, they are more than amply rewarded. The forgotten majority is a large and fast-growing market. Because of cultural differences, geographical distances, and differences in needs and economic capabilities, among others, companies may not have an easy time marketing products and services in these markets. However, the pay-off can be great due to the fact that global giants ignore these markets, thereby eliminating competition. In addition, if companies can introduce reasonable and attractive products and services into these markets, consumers will buy them quickly and become loyal customers.

THE WORLD'S LARGEST MARKETS

You should not get the idea that these large markets are one huge, identifiable, and homogeneous market. On the contrary, even though the forgotten majority represents a very large market, it is composed of thousands of sites scattered all over the world, made up of people speaking hundreds of different languages, and made up of hundreds of different cultural backgrounds affecting the behavior pattern and (perhaps, above all) the wealth of individuals. Although they are mostly poor, these markets are showings signs of progress, growth, and dynamism. Sooner or later their needs must be at least nominally satisfied, which is where the challenge and profit potential lies.

THE WORLD'S LARGEST MARKETS ARE ON THE MARCH

Even though, economically, the poor markets of the world may not be keeping up with the growth rates and growth patterns of the G-7 countries (the seven largest industrial economies in the world) and other countries, third-world markets are on the march. They are very familiar with the goods and services that their counterparts in developed corners of the world are enjoying. These poorer consumers may not have Mercedes-Benzes or BMWs, but they are becoming aware of the importance of getting from Point A to Point B perhaps with a bicycle or a motorcycle—in other words, faster. Consumers in third-world countries (through exposure to movies; newspapers; television; and, to a limited extent, computers) are familiar with what is happening in industrialized countries and the lifestyles prevailing in these places. This makes these consumers anxious to improve their own lives by buying more products and services.

Large segments of third-world populations are young and more ambitious about having a better life through goods and services. Consumers in these countries are craving more and better goods and services. Although still quite stagnant, third-world markets, in a sporadic manner, are showing signs of growth. And those vast parts of the world that can be described primarily by the presence of economic stagnation are experiencing a ripple effect from ongoing globalization. In other words, directly or indirectly, select positive economic activity, primarily due to globalization, is influencing many parts of economically stagnant areas with economic activity and with heightened aspirations. As mentioned earlier, one of the key considerations regarding third-world markets is that competition is not very advanced, meaning there are many opportunities for small and medium companies. Not needing to worry about competition, these companies can instead, worry about satisfying the modest demands of various small consumer groups. This is a risky proposition, but so is functioning on the fringes of Western markets, which are run by oligopolistic giants and are somewhat saturated (Samli 2000).

THE SIZE OF THE FORGOTTEN MAJORITY MARKET

Just how big are the markets within which the forgotten majority functions? The less developed markets of the world are sizable. Figure Intro-1 presents estimates of the U.S. market, the European Union market, and the less developed markets of the world. The third-world markets combined are larger than the U.S. market and European Union market individually or combined. Understand, however, that the $16 trillion market of the third-world countries represents about 90 percent of the world 's population and perhaps more than two-thirds of the world's geography. Although the calculations were made as of

Figure Intro-1. The Size of World Markets (mid 2001)

The size of less developed markets	$16,315,200,000,000
The size of the U.S. market	$ 9,078,395,000,000
The size of the European Union market	$ 6,747,959,000,000

Note: Income figures are based on purchasing power parity (PPP). By using PPP, incomes are made comparable.

Source: Calculated by the author based on population and income figures reported in *World Population Data Sheet*, http://www.http://www.prb.org.

mid-2001, the expected growth of the European Union's membership would not be significantly different than what is calculated here.

FORTRESS EUROPE VERSUS BAMBOO INDONESIA OR MALAYSIA

With globalization efforts, the markets of Europe and particularly North America have become very competitive. Thus, Fortress Europe and Fortress North America cannot be considered easy markets to enter. However, whereas developed markets of the world can be seen as fortresses, developing and less developed markets of the world can be seen as being surrounded with loose bamboo fences.

Countries such as Indonesia, Malaysia, and others with checkered performance records with regard to economic development, but anxious to improve the quality of life for their citizens, are quite open to doing business, consuming certain products and services, and getting their societies on a track of growth and improvement. Hence, with less effort (but perhaps more dedication and slightly heightened risk), doing business in these ignored or forgotten markets can be successful and profitable.

Some years ago Nwachukwu and Dant (1990) maintained that consumers in many different cultures in the world are similar in more ways than one usually considers. Such a way of thinking may imply that what one does in Market A can easily be done in Market B. However, that is not the case. Here Markets A and B may be very different and, therefore, must be treated accordingly. The key in dealing successfully with small markets is emphasizing the differences, not the similarities. Small entrepreneurial firms can do this, international giants cannot.

IT IS NOT THE SIMILARITIES BUT THE DIFFERENCES THAT COUNT

Every culture has its uniqueness that influences values, communications, behavior patterns, aspirations, acquisitions, and accomplishments. The forgotten markets of the world are extremely multicultural. Thus, if businesses approach these markets as if they are all the same or at least very similar, the businesses will lose. Levitt (1983) discussed what he termed "the new commercial reality," which he described as "the explosive emergence of global markets for globally standardized products, gigantic world-scale market of previously unimagined magnitudes." Indeed, these markets are already in existence and they are huge. However, in this book, the discussion is about something dramatically different. The forgotten majority is very different from the gigantic world-scale market demanding globally standardized products. There is no critical mass for standardized products. Markets are very sketchy and diverse, behavior patterns are varied, and marketing practices must be different in each of these difficult-to-identify and demanding small markets. Thus, the global giants' loss is small and medium size companies gain.

If you look at these small markets in greater detail, you can see that notable and significant differences are important. Companies in small markets are all different and do not require standardized products. In short, one size does not fit all. Such a proposition is agreeable for small- and medium-size companies that are flexible. These small companies do not thrive on selling standardized products in large quantities using the same marketing approaches and treating consumers the same wherever and whoever they are.

The differences and the cultural diversity in the forgotten or ignored markets of the world do count; the differences exist and must be addressed. Moreover, those flexible and understanding companies that cater to the needs of the forgotten majority are likely to profit financially as well as spread much happiness. This book discusses some of the major differences in needs and behavior patterns that result in these consumers from extremely varied backgrounds eventually becoming recognized. When companies acknowledge the recognizable differences, they can sell goods and services in these markets that make a difference in terms of consumer satisfaction and commensurate profitability. In other words, consumers or members of the forgotten majority appreciate having their acute need for goods and services satisfied. Such gratification, by definition, translates into profits for those companies that are daring enough to cater to the forgotten majority. Those companies that are daring, that are risk takers, and who have compassion and ambition must be cognizant of how they fit into these third-world markets. Global giants cannot deal with these small and extremely scattered markets; however, given certain behavior patterns, small- and medium-size firms can be very profitable in forgotten markets.

MACRO-ORIENTATION IS NECESSARY

Many third-world markets are fragile. Therefore, it is almost impossible to take without giving. In other words, if a company wants to make money, it must consider the market's well-being; that is, it must generate consumer value in return for its profit. If transactions generated by a company, either domestic or international, do not create some degree of vitality in these markets, the markets may not survive. If they don't survive, the company also loses.

Making an ally out of a potential obstacle is the philosophical way of dealing with the forgotten majority. In third-world countries, on average, consumers own much less than their Western and North American counterparts. Therefore, third-world consumers' interest in a product is usually very high and their unsatisfied needs are more pronounced.

Although individual interest in a product by that market is critical, the impact of the product from a macroperspective also counts; a product desired by consumers should also help the local economy. If, for instance, consumers are interested in asbestos but they do not know the product causes asbestosis (a deadly lung disease), the product is not good for the market. For some short-run profit, long-term consumer values should not be sacrificed. A healthy and growing market yields more profit in the long run than a windfall profit in the short run.

Figure Intro-2 illustrates the connection of a product to the individual and to the economy. If a company can sell a product that appeals to local customers and that makes a modest economic contribution, the result is a synergistic impact; therefore, the company does well.

At least three features of a product must be considered from both micro- and macroperspectives: physical, economic and psychological.

Physical Features: Appearance, size, package durability, performance, and need satisfaction are all physical features. Ap-

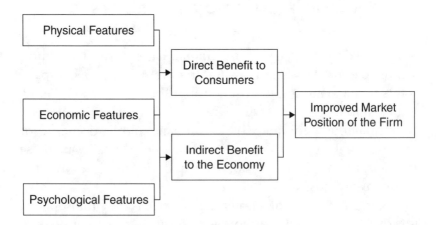

Figure Intro-2. Impact of Product

pearances are important, particularly to those who have little to show. An appearance preference, therefore, is real and very cultural. Consumer culture is variable at the local level and may vary even more significantly within a region. Therein lies one of the advantages of having a small- or medium-size company. Very large global firms cannot cope with local idiosyncrasies and cannot produce small quantities for different markets. They must take advantage of economies of scale.

Size has many implications in terms of satisfying consumer needs. Most consumers in emerging markets or third-world countries live in very small quarters. They do not have extra space for bulky products. However, within that constraint, the sizes can vary significantly. These are key reasons why large corporations that prefer limited variations and large quantities do not look at these small and variable markets. These markets simply do not represent the critical volume potential large companies need to function profitably. Package plays a critical role in different cultures. For example, consider the Japanese orientation: if there is a problem with packaging, there is a good chance something is wrong with the contents too. In other cultures, the package or the container is used for a variety of purposes, something that large global firms would have difficulty delivering.

Durability is critical in third-world markets and for the forgotten majority. Since these consumes do not have enough purchasing power to buy a variety of things and to replace them, whatever the people buy in these countries must last a very long time. The global giants, on the other hand, thrive on changing model and making existing products obsolete.

Performance of a product is important to consumers looking to make a purchase. Having a limited income and not being able to returning a product in many parts of the world, consumers must make sure the product performs as expected. Once again, the global giants do not worry much about the performance factor because their products are standardized; these companies do not cater to important differences that exist in different parts of poor countries.

Closely related to performance is need satisfaction. The forgotten majorities may be poor, but they have highly varying and relatively well-articulated needs. But because of the limited demand, global companies ignore these markets and their needs.

Macro-Implications: These physical features, in addition to their direct contribution to consumers' well-being, also have indirect macro-implications. Above all, any contribution in the production or distribution of products domestically may make a major contribution to the local economy. Naturally, while partial production of a small firm's output does not make a major impact in the industrialization of a third-world country, output can still make a reasonable and valuable contribution.

Another macro-implication relates to improved choices for consumers. When a company's products meet specific needs, consumers do not need to search other products to find what they are looking for. This frees consumers from running around and looking helplessly for those products. Thus, more time and fewer pressures can significantly impact consumers' activity, allowing them to deal with other issues and work on other projects.

Resource utilization is another macro-implication. For example, if a company develops a little attachment that allows existing cars to use alcohol, in Cuba, this may mean a rather important use of the sugar industry, which has been stagnant lately. Cubans can save their limited foreign exchange and buy more important industrial products that help the country's economy grow.

In addition to choice, availability can make a better contribution to the economic well-being. In a culture dependent upon bicycles, the introduction of special electric bikes that generate electricity by pedaling can be rather significant if people's efficiency is enhanced because they can move faster. The local economy would benefit from such a product.

Economic Features:
Since third-world countries have limited per capita incomes, products entering these markets must be reasonably priced. This way, products can penetrate these limited but important

markets, giving consumers the opportunity to buy other products as well. The perceived value of products for those people who have very little is substantial, and consumers who buy these products believe they are economically better off. Since large global firms are more interested in profit per unit, they are not interested in low-priced products. Therefore, these third-world markets are forgotten.

Macro-Implications:

Macro-implications of economic features can be many. First, availability and affordability of certain products can improve consumer health and give consumers more energy and peace of mind. All of these factors can improve the productivity of a consumer who is a worker in, say, a factory. Second, when some products coming into a country use local raw materials, parts, or components (or even if the products are only assembled locally), more jobs become available the economic base expands. Third, when some technologies, however small-scale they may be, are transferred, a ripple effect is likely to occur. Know-how learned from one technology spills over to others, and the economy benefits indirectly.

Psychological Features:

Some brands and/or some products in third-world countries become so important they are almost legendary. When people do not own much, ownership of a brand or product creates "ownership utility." Thus, psychological features of products can be very positive. American-made products in Mexico have such general stature. A Singer sewing machine can be the focal point of a household. Country of origin (COO) identification can have a special psychological meaning that makes consumers in less developed markets quite happy.

Many global giants do not pay attention to the ownership preferences of the poorer markets. Because these markets are not very profitable, larger companies stay out of these areas. Stated differently, corporate giants cannot afford to be very sensitive to the varying needs of small and scattered markets of emerging countries.

In terms of macro-implications, if ownership of certain products in a market or region creates a positive attitude toward life, those products are likely to be important to the economy.

WHY SMALL- AND MEDIUM-SIZE COMPANIES?

The majority of people in the world are rather poor; are scattered; and have varied tastes, needs, and behavior patterns. As a result, the global giant corporations have forgotten them. However, much market potential is represented by the forgotten majority. After all, the consumers in poorer countries also have needs. Although somewhat meager, these consumers also have some purchasing power. For medium and small companies, these conditions can be quite suitable and profitable. This book is based on this premise. Since large corporations have forgotten these consumers, only small- and medium-size companies are likely to deal with marginal markets. Because of their versatility and flexibility, small and medium firms can cater to these markets rather successfully.

READING THROUGH THIS BOOK

Following is a brief synopsis of each chapter.
- The forgotten majority resides in emerging world markets. As a total, these areas represent very large and growing markets. (Introduction)
- Globalization cannot be sustained unless a second wave of globalization takes place, addressing the forgotten majority. (Chapter 1)
- This second wave of globalization and successful marketing to the forgotten majority can be accomplished only by small- and medium-size enterprises. They are flexible, agile, and closer to the markets. (Chapter 2)
- In the forgotten majority markets, consumers differ from their counterparts in industrialized markets. Consumers' needs and behaviors are varied and nonstandardized.

Forgotten majority markets are small and scattered. Because these markets are scattered and because cultural differences exist, understanding how consumers behave and what their needs are becomes very important. (Chapter 3)

- Because of existing emotionalism and because of the scattered nature of markets in third-world countries, companies must learn to negotiate with the forgotten majorities located in target markets. These target markets must be chosen from numerous possible market segments. (Chapter 4)
- No matter how anxious a company may be to enter the emerging markets of third-world countries, unless the company a partner, it cannot succeed. With this partner, the company must develop a mutually advantageous, strategic, and synergistic alliance. (Chapter 5)
- All alliances are not quite strategic. A company must make sure the alliance it creates with a partner is strategic. (Chapter 6)
- Unless a company has a product or service that the target market finds not only desirable but also essential, the company is not likely to be successful. (Chapter 7)
- Having a good product is critical, but in these less developed and scattered markets, physically reaching the consumer is an even greater challenge. (Chapter 8)
- As merchandise moves through unusual channels of distribution in third-world countries, companies must attempt to communicate with their consumers. Communication with the market segments is a special responsibility of companies. (Chapter 9)
- Generating consumer value is particularly critical in third-world countries, where money is scarce and consumer needs are plentiful. Therefore, the pricing of products takes on a new and different meaning. (Chapter 10)
- Everything a company does in its target markets can be labeled the implementation of a strategy. Companies have had different strategies before. In this case, however, a company must make sure its strategy is adjusted to poorer markets. (Chapter 11)

- Despite all marketing activity and partnering, a company is still an independent entity. It is calling the shots. The company must be entrepreneurial, and the alliance it creates must be entrepreneurial as well. (Chapter 12)
- If a company wants to create a truly entrepreneurial and synergistic alliance that is a necessity to the forgotten majority, the company must be understanding and fair with its partners. (Chapter 13)
- Since conditions can change quickly in the markets where the forgotten majority is located, a company must monitor its activities and market conditions continuously. (Chapter 14)
- Looking toward the future, international entrepreneurship plays an important role in remembering the forgotten majority. (Chapter 15)

SUMMARY

The majority of people in the world are poor. But these consumers represent large markets. Global giant corporations ignore them. Entering these markets and catering to their needs is not easy.

Marginal markets of the world are composed of many markets that have different cultural, ethnic, and behavioral aspects. There is no critical mass in terms of total demand (if any demand) attractive enough to a global firm. But that demand is attractive to small- or medium-size firms.

Since Fortress Europe is taken by global giants, Bamboo Indonesia, for example, may be examined as a potential market.

Cultural diversity of these forgotten markets reflects on the products they need with regard to three key sets of features: physical, economic, and psychological. The variety and clear-cut differences in the products demanded by these markets make them easily forgotten by global giants.

The Second Wave of Globalization

G lobalization has been going on for a long time. Deregulation, decentralization, privatization, and the development of cyberspace in the 1980s and 1990s have paved the way to globalization during the past two decades. Friedman (2000) described globalization as an "electronic herd." Perhaps the most important fact about this herd is that its speed is accelerating. Samli also discussed four flows that are further accelerating the globalization process: the flow of information, the flow of technology, the financial flow, and the flow of human know-how.

The preceding four developments (i.e., deregulation, decentralization, privatization, and the development of cyberspace) made free trade and the transfer of technology possible. The subsequent four flows kept accelerating the globalization process. The end result is that although some groups, some countries, and some businesses benefit immensely, globally the economic gap between haves and have-nots is becoming wider. The outcome of these ongoing series of events is that the electronic herd is moving faster, creating more trade opportunities for some people, but also leaving other people behind. Thus, only some, in fact only a few, are with the herd that is taking over, meaning that not enough trade opportunities are being taken advantage of.

The key world markets in Western and Northern Europe, North America, Japan and a few other places are attracting global firms to enter and conduct business. But much of the rest of the world is ignored. As the electronic herd takes over these core markets, the remainder of the world's markets are stagnating. They are not participating in and receiving a fair share from this first wave of globalization. Therefore, there is a need for a second wave of globalization. The second wave of globalization takes the globalization process to smaller lesser-developed markets via smaller entrepreneurial companies. These companies enter secondary and tertiary markets of third-world countries. As smaller companies help these markets to globalize, they transfer technology; they also make money in these marginal or niche markets where little competition exists. Small entrepreneurial businesses of the West can profit financially as they generate consumer value by broadening the outreach of this much-needed second wave of globalization.

Third-world markets have much to offer to those companies who want to do business there, and it is almost a foregone conclusion that third-world markets will wake up to the trade opportunities that can benefit all parties involved. If companies reach out and help these markets become part of the globalization process, they will create consumer value and make a profit. This second wave of globalization can have a tremendous impact on global trade and world economies.

THIRD WORLD HAS MUCH TO OFFER

What the third world has to offer can be analyzed from a supply perspective as well as from a demand perspective. The following is a brief description of each.

In terms of supply, many developed countries are either running out of scarce resources or are finding it too costly to use these resources. America is importing more petroleum that ever before. Japan is dependent on iron ore and petroleum, to name a few. Many third-world countries are capable of supplying raw materials, semifinished products, parts, or components, often becoming the outsourcing targets of industrialized countries. Thus, joint ventures between companies from the industrialized world and third-world countries become feasible in order to use international sourcing appropriately. Joint venturing and outsourcing will likely go on indefinitely emerging more in third-world markets than other places. The reason is because, in most cases, natural resources in third-world countries are not yet widely used, but are being developed.

In terms of demand, third-world countries have a lot to offer. Generally, expenditures on basic necessities are higher in these countries. People spend proportionately more money on food, household items, transportation, apparel, and footwear. People also, relatively speaking, spend less on entertainment, medical care, and rent. But outside of these general areas, consumers in third-world markets buy almost everything else, just slowly and in much smaller quantities. In other words, bec\ause they have limited incomes, consumers insist on getting more value for their money and they buy things gradually. They may not buy luxury cars or luxury bicycles, but they do buy quality products that are reasonably priced.

Durability of products is particularly critical. In some parts of Turkey, for instance, the word for refrigerator is *Frigidaire*, and people brag about how long they have had their unit. A private brand such as Frigidaire can be so popular that it becomes a generic name. If such a unit is purchased, it is obtained through sacrifice by saving. Therefore, the item is considered almost a lifetime investment.

If a company has difficulty selling one unit, why should the business bother with such a market? The answer is rather simple. Many people live in these markets, and they need goods and services. Sooner or later their needs surface. Hence, producing and selling reasonably priced, long-lasting products actually helps the domestic economies of these countries, in addition to satisfying consumer needs. Opportunities like this are likely to emerge very often as the first wave of globalization continues to accelerate. These marginal or submarginal markets are small, but totally untapped. No competition exists and consumer needs are not taken care of. Untapped markets mean profit for those who participate in them.

GLOBALIZATION IS INEVITABLE

The first wave, or perhaps first tier, of globalization has been and is going on. It is gaining momentum and accelerating. Despite local demonstrations and loud objections, globalization will continue. Many authors have raised the sustainability issue of globalization as the first wave continues. Technology is passed on to a privileged few, capital is transferred to a privileged few, information is given to a privileged few, and skills are transferred to a privileged few. Thus, haves become have-mores and have-nots become have-nothing (Samli 2002). In other words, the gap between the rich and the poor is widening. Such a pattern sheds doubt on just how sustainable globalization is.

But stopping globalization abruptly and artificially has no value either. Globalization may be the only way third-world countries have a chance to develop their economies. Instead of avoiding globalization, these countries should find a way to participate in the process gainfully. This can be achieved by developing partnerships, networks, and trading blocs and participating in the second-, third-, and fourth-tier world markets productively and gainfully.

DEVELOPING PARTNERSHIPS, NETWORKS, AND TRADING BLOCS:

Companies in third-world markets want to actively participate in the globalization process. As a result, Western small- and medium-size companies have an opportunity to expand into international markets. Companies from third-world markets can become a part of globalization by developing or participating in partnerships, networks, and trading blocs.

Figure 1-1 illustrates a seven-step process that will enable companies in less developed markets to become active participants in the globalization process. Keep in mind that these companies are not necessarily from third-world countries; these businesses may be from developed parts of the world that want to expand into other parts of the world. At the writing of this book, Nokia, the Finnish manufacturer of cell phones, is looking to outsource all of its output outside of Finland. Also, many American companies are moving to Mexico or partnering with Mexican companies. These are only two examples of widespread global activity.

The first step in Figure 1-1 is identifying partnership possibilities. Companies from the industrialized world look at such opportunities differently than their counterparts in third-world countries. (This is discussed further in Chapter 4.) Identifying partnership possibilities automatically leads to finding partners. So partnership areas must be carefully identified and prioritized and appropriate partners must be found. Finding appropriate partners is as difficult as, if not more, difficult than, the first step.

Finding the right partner, if done properly, allows the partners to work in a synchronized manner. This partnership benefits both parties and, in a sense, makes the activity synergistic.

Having just one or two partners may not be enough. If growth were to take place, the partnership would expand into a network with multiple partners in different regions or in different neighboring countries. A group of small textile manufacturers in Turkey, for instance, may organize a group of exporters jointly. A U.S. firm that becomes part of this group or a similar network can benefit significantly. Joint networks can buy or sell a variety of products or services. They are substantially more powerful than a simple partnership.

Defining which company plays what kind of a role in a network becomes a critical issue. The network must have a strategy of its own that does not clash with the strategies of its members.

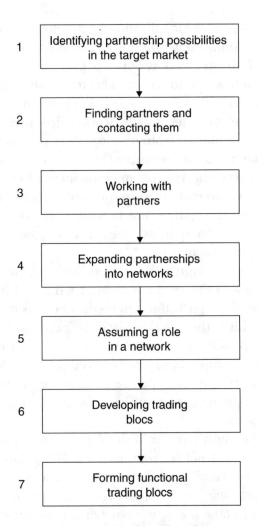

Figure 1-1. From Partnerships to Trading Blocs Steps

> **Note:** Although many textbooks and other sources consider trading blocs as govern-
> ment-developed entities, in this book, the term is treated as multiple trading networks.
> The author of this book has seen such networks functioning successfully as blocs for
> both buyers and sellers.

Not only is it necessary to determine who does what in a network, it is also necessary to assess the changes in these functions and their effectiveness. Networks aiming primarily at
marginal markets of the third world are not quite yet developed. However, their time is coming.

If and when networks can be expanded into trading blocs, as in step 6 of Figure 1-1, the power base becomes even more significant. Having multiple networks trading with other multiple networks can play a significant role in regional development. No hard-and-fast criteria exist as to the size of a trading bloc versus a network. Typically, though, as a group of networks (say, a group of Greek merchants) begins trading with a network (say, German and French businesses), trading blocs are in action. Just as in partnerships and networks, trading blocks need to be ongoing entities; they must trade continuously. These trading blocs must be functional in that they generate benefit for all parties involved. The seven-step process described in Figure 1-1 makes it very plausible for small Western firms to become hooked up with companies from third-world countries. In other words, this process is the foundation of what may be called a second-tier globalization.

POTENTIAL FOR SECOND- AND THIRD-TIER GLOBALIZATION

As has been discussed, globalization is taking place. However, it is leaving behind the majority of the world's population and the majority of the world's nations. The second- and third-tier globalization activity, also called the second wave of globalization, is a must if globalization as a whole can be fair and sustainable (Samli 2002). This second- and third-tier globalization is not likely take place mostly in third-world countries, outside of key global markets; however, it is likely be initiated by companies from third-world countries, although exceptions will occur. By the same token, multi-national giants do not deviate from the industrialized world markets (or perhaps the first tier in the emerging markets). Corporate giants enter the markets from the high end and are engaged only in niche marketing for the rich. Therefore, chances are that only small- and medium-size American and Western firms will generate the whole second wave of globalization activity, perhaps starting with simple exports to tiers two and three. These firms must have a certain management orientation that will make the second wave of globalization successful. They will not follow the corporate imperialism that selectively favors only rich markets.

MANAGEMENT ORIENTATION IN THE SECOND WAVE

Since the late 1970s, hardly a community in the United States would not encourage international trading, exporting, or enticing foreign investments. Indeed, many communities, in order to stimulate international trade, exporting, and foreign investments, have developed *home-front alliances* that are connected to *target market alliances*. Much of the time, local alliances find prospective exporters or international participants and help these firms get started. Both home-front and target market alliances must combine to perform certain basic international trade supporting functions. Without such action trade will be impeded and the second wave of globalization may not get started.

Figure 1-2 shows how these support systems come into being and how they overcome rather obvious impediments. Functions and impediments are briefly discussed below.

Assume, for instance, that a small canned food producer from Jacksonville, Florida, decides to begin marketing in central Africa. The prospective exporter may not have enough resources and/or the know-how to function successfully in the target market. The home-front alliance generates and provides leads as to where, who, and what. Without these leads, the potential exporter will not be able to take advantage of international opportunities. The alliance provides target market information, in this case going beyond where, who, and what. The alliance provides information about economic conditions, market potentials, and growth possibilities—without which the Florida canned food producer would have little or no target market information. The alliance also provides a

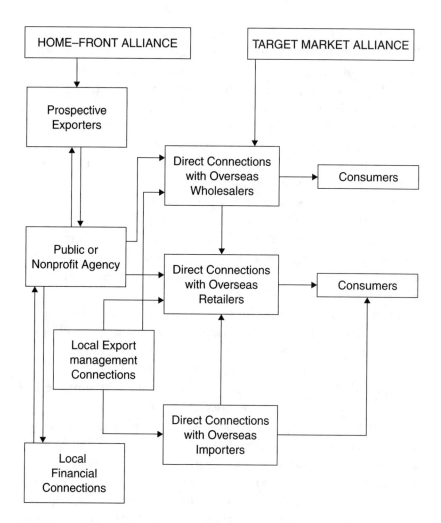

Figure 1-2 Model for an Export Support System.

Note: The term *Public or Nonprofit Agency* refers to a formal, semiformal, or informal local network, which is functioning as a strategic alliance.

directory of names of possible importers or partners—without which the Florida canned food producer would have no local contacts. The home-front part of the alliance becomes engaged in overseas networking with prospective contacts in central Africa. Without such involvement, the canned food producer would have no opportunity to proceed. The alliance also explores the possibility of eliminating the government red tape (if any exists) for both sides. The red tape, particularly in less developed countries, can be rather involved. Logistics-related problems are often critical in international marketing activities, and the alliance explores the most practical alternatives. Logistics in a third-world country can be rather limited because of scarcity of transportation or warehousing alternatives, and the prospective Florida exporter needs assistance. Finally, the alliance provides financial information as well as connections. Without financial support and assurance, the canned food processor cannot function in the target market. The home-front alliance, if it is hooked up with a target market alliance, allows international transactions to move very smoothly. The target market alliance, as shown in Figure 1-2, is connected to direct importers or distributors and can do the marketing activity at that end.

Thus, management in the second wave is greatly empowered by an export or international trade support system. Such a system is composed of a home-front alliance and a target market alliance (Samli 1996), as illustrated in Figure 1-2.

In the final analysis, the home-front alliance is composed of a support system for the prospective exporter or the international trade. This support system may include nonprofit organizations such as the Chamber of Commerce, the Mayor's Commission for International Trade, or a local branch of the Department of Commerce. A local export management company and a local or regional bank may be part of the alliance. In the target market alliance, wholesalers, retailers, or importers may be included. Above all, a local contact organization is the key for success.

An export or international trade support system is critical in the needed forthcoming second wave of globalization. Exporting and international trade are used interchangeably because, for instance, the Florida canned food processor can easily expand its business to outsource from the region, develop an assembly line in the area, or start a joint venture and market in other countries of the region. The critical factor is just to start the whole process rolling.

Management orientation in the second wave is proactive, as it was in the first wave. However, this proactive approach must be nourished by export support systems. Entering smaller and perhaps less profitable world markets that exist in third-world countries requires a push before the proactive orientation emerges. Considering the fact that the proposed market opportunities are more appropriate for small and medium companies, this push is especially critical because many of these companies have not even thought of entering international markets.

The markets where the forgotten majority lives are not only sizable, as was discussed earlier, but are also growing. Above all, they are almost totally untapped because global giants prefer large global markets.

THE GROWTH IN WORLD MARKETS

Figure 1-3 illustrates rather encouraging growth patterns for some of the marginal markets of the world. In almost all cases, the growth rates in the developing world as a whole have been greater than the developed Western Hemisphere—an estimated growth rate of over 4 percent. The Asian and Russian republics (Commonwealth of Independent States) appear to be growing at even healthier rates. Despite the fact that inflation is a reality in many of these countries, there is still substantial real growth and, therefore, great opportunity, particularly for small- and medium-size Western firms. Figure 1-3 shows that the chances are very good that the second-, third- and fourth-tier markets around the world will grow much faster than the industrialized and first-tier markets.

Some estimates indicate that by 2010, ten developing countries will account for more than 40 percent of all global imports. These countries are Argentina, Brazil, Mexico, China, Indonesia, India, Poland, South Korea, South Africa, and Turkey. Six industry clusters are identified as most promising

Figure 1-3. Comparison of Growth of GDP*

	Real GDP			
	1999	2000	2001	2002
Developing World	3.9	5.8	4.0	4.4
Africa	2.5	2.8	3.5	3.5
Developing Asia	6.2	6.8	5.6	5.6
Middle East	3.0	5.5	4.5	3.8
Western Hemisphere	0.1	4.1	1.0	1.7
EU Accession Candidates	---	4.8	0.2	3.4
Commonwealth of Independent States	4.6	7.9	6.1	3.9

Source: IMF World Outlook, Chapter 3: Global and Regional Economic Prospects, 2001.

*Figures represent percentage change for each particular year

for export promotion: environmental technologies, information technologies, health technologies, transportation technologies, energy technologies, and financial services (Business America 1994). One can easily foresee the spillover of these industry clusters into many varieties of local businesses, carrying the benefits of these dynamic sectors far into remote corners of third-world markets. This book posits that the second wave of globalization will expand into all aspects of consumer products and services. Indeed, in a broader sense, the second wave of globalization will add a much-needed sustainability feature to the current globalization process.

SUMMARY

This chapter poses a critical issue of sustained globalization. The way the first wave of globalization is progressing, there is clearly a need for a second wave. This second wave deals with the forgotten majority. Third-world countries and their markets have tremendous potential. However, major global firms mostly ignore them. The void here can be easily eliminated by medium and small firms on both sides—the industrialized world and the third-world. Third-world markets can provide supplies, participate in joint ventures, or accommodate Western companies' attempts to outsource.

Third-world markets have demands not as powerful and colorful as industrialized markets, but still large and varied. There is a need not for luxury, but for quality and durable products that are reasonably priced. The need must be addressed.

A Western firm can enter these markets in a progressive manner, starting with simple exports, developing partnerships, moving in the direction of networking, and creating trading blocs. As a result, a second-tier globalization is likely to emerge. Because the neglected majority becomes a part of globalization and begins to benefit from it, globalization as a whole becomes more sustainable and has a very positive future.

For the second wave of globalization to be successful, management on both sides must be proactive. Both parties must initiate the trade activity and make sure it is continuing. Initiation and continuity of the trade activity is heavily dependent upon the creation of export or trade support systems that are local, functioning, and location-specific. These support systems have two components, home-front alliance and target market alliance. If these alliances work in unison and function effectively, most likely the second wave will run smoothly.

Finally, the markets where the forgotten majority functions are growing. Although not attractive to global giants, third-world markets are promising for small- and medium-size companies of the West.

REFERENCES

Business America (1994). "The Big Emerging Markets," Oct., 59–66.

Friedman, Thomas (2000). *Lexus and Olive Tree*, New York: Anchor Books.

Samli, A. Coskun (1996). *International Consumer Behavior*, Westport, Connecticut: Quorum Books.

Samli, A. Coskun (2002). *In Search of a Fair, Sustainable Globalization*. Westport, Connecticut: Quorum Books.

2

What Small- and Medium-Size Enterprises Have to Offer International Markets

A company such as IBM, Dell, or Xerox may not give a second thought to the fact that there may be a very modest, slowly growing, and still quite poor market for their products in southeast Turkey. In addition to being rather small (and therefore not having the necessary critical mass for a worthwhile market), this market is composed of varied needs, behavior patterns, and purchase behaviors. Thus, the market is not very profitable and it is difficult for companies to function there. But this is primarily so only for global giants. General Electric, Gillette, and General Foods may not be concerned about Congolese consumers who wait for their income from their annual cash crops so they can go to a city six hours away to buy canned food, powdered milk, medicine, clothing, furniture, bikes, watches, sewing machines, and radios. But small entrepreneurial businesses can export, assemble, and produce many of these products through collaboration with local partners. In the process, these companies profit financially; they create more localized consumer value.

This is the general picture of the markets where the forgotten majority lives. Global giants have difficulty dealing with these markets because they are not profitable enough; hence, they are not attractive. Kellogg, for example, found that introducing breakfast cereals to the Indian market was a very slow process because people's eating habits were hard to break. The company could not offer breakfast cereals with local flavors; it was too costly. The consumer education activity also proved very costly. Kellogg discovered that it paid too high a price for too small a market (Prahalad and Lieberthal 1998).

But the story is different for small- and medium-size companies. They can function rather easily in these markets, and these markets can be quite profitable for them. Small- and medium-size companies do not need to support large organizational bureaucracies; they do not spend much on research and development; and above all, they are not accountable to large groups of investors. They can do well with smaller returns on investments. Thus, some small- or medium-size firms may be attracted to the slowly emerging market of southeast Turkey or any part of the third world market. Why is it that small- and medium-size firms can function in marginal or submarginal markets?

SPECIAL STRENGTHS OF SMALL- AND MEDIUM-SIZE FIRMS

Small- and medium-size companies have an advantage over large global giants in at least four areas: innovativeness, flexibility, closeness to the market, and participation in joint activity.

Figure 2-1 illustrates the four features that make small and medium firms more suitable to enter third-world markets where the forgotten majority lives.

INNOVATIVENESS

Small- and medium-size firms may not have many research resources, but when it comes to creativity, they can accomplish a lot. First of all, they can generate new ideas or new ways of using old ideas. Although old-fashioned crank-type washers have not been used in the West for over 40 years, a company has produced them for parts of the third world where energy and water are not plentiful. The product has been a great success. This is an example of using an old idea very creatively. Second, small- and medium-size companies can explore opportunities closely. Whereas 50 specific tractors for Nepal may not be an attractive deal for International Harvester, a small company from Belarus can easily accommodate the order. Third, small and medium companies are interested in and practice nonconventional behavior. A German manufacturer of appliances took a Turkish company to court for pirating its products. It won the case. The Turkish company subsequently received a phone call from the German company. The message was as follows: "Why don't we merge? Your products are as good as ours, but much cheaper. You make them and we'll market them." That is a nonconventional and innovative approach. Fourth, small and medium companies are internally cohesive, meaning no internal hierarchies exist where communications and activities must go through multiple layers, often resulting in derailment or delays. In smaller firms, everyone is part of the decision/action process and involved in trying to make the firm functional.

FLEXIBILITY

One of the major traits of smaller firms is that they are flexible. This feature surfaces in many different ways. Some of them are presented in Figure 2-1.

Whereas large firms cannot make sudden changes in their strategies, in their product mixes, or in their target market decisions, smaller firms can easily make sudden decisions and implement them quickly. Doing so gives an edge to these firms since they are dealing with rather changeable and unpredictable markets.

Making sudden changes in practices includes going in the opposite direction (or at least making some change in direction). This kind of practice is nearly impossible for large firms. In the late 1980s, Parker pens wanted to imitate BIC. The company came up with a "one-cheap-model-fits-all" design, but the

Figure 2-1. Features of Small- and Medium-Size International Companies

1. Innovativeness
   a. Generating new ideas
   b. Exploring opportunities
   c. Having an interest in nonconventional behaviors
   d. Having internal cohesiveness

2. Flexibility
   a. Can make sudden changes
   b. Can change direction
   c. Can make dramatically different plans
   d. Can make major decisions very quickly

3. Closeness to the market
   a. Understanding market conditions
      i. Change in competition
      ii. Change in consumer desires
      iii. Change in the economy
      iv. Change in government policies
   b. Being sensitive to consumer needs
   c. Understanding how consumers behave
   d. Being able to enter a market first

4. Participation in joint activity
   a. Finding partners
   b. Becoming part of networks
   c. Working closely with other supporting networks
   d. Finding trading blocs to work with

product received a financial beating. The company could not stop or reverse this losing proposition. In the late 1990s. Benetton initiated a series of controversial advertisements. In many parts of the world, public opinion turned against the company. As a result, Benetton's profit picture did not appear too attractive. It took quite a long time for the company to reverse this trend.

Small international firms are flexible enough to make dramatically different plans from their current onoing activities. A medium-size American wholesaler of food products entered the Russian market on a limited scale using a local intermediary. Then the company realized that the intermediary was limiting its entry and sales in the market. The wholesaler decided to bypass the intermediary so it could become more active and independent in the growing Russian market. Such possibilities are commonplace in the world of the forgotten majority.

Finally, smaller flexible firms can make decisions very quickly. Atlas International Company, an export management company, by keeping abreast with the changes in overseas markets, has managed to give efficient service to its customers. Its customers, therefore, are able to make quick and effective decisions about their export activity.

CLOSENESS TO THE MARKET

Smaller firms have a greater opportunity to be close to the market and understand the conditions that exist in these markets. If the prevailing market conditions change, the firms can quickly adjust and act accordingly. Figure 2-1 presents four types of changes in the conditions that exist in the market: competition, consumer desires, the economy, and government policies.

If a company is not very close to the market, it may not sense changes in competition quickly enough to make needed critical adjustments. Similarly, without being close to the market, a company may not see a change in consumer desires. Economic conditions, particularly in third-world countries, may change rather unexpectedly. Being close to the market enables a company to detect the changes in the economy and their extensiveness. Finally, governments in third-world countries may make important changes influencing how business is conducted in their markets. A company may not be able to detect these changes from a distance. Being close to the market becomes a critical asset so a company can use these changes in its best interest.

Consumer needs can vary significantly from one market to the next. If a firm does not understand consumer needs, it cannot make progress. Smaller firms are close to the market and, hence, are likely to be more sensitive to varying consumer needs. Large global companies act more monopolistically in that they take the attitude of "Well, this is what we have. Take it or leave it."

International giants are often insensitive to consumer needs and don't understand how consumers behave. After the fall of the Berlin Wall, for instance, Westerners assumed that consumers from the East would be anxious to buy their products. Consumers did not appear to switch to new and better brands. Not only were the products high-priced, but Easterners did not have much money. Also, the products had multiple features, the benefits of which were not known to consumers. Consumers were confused about additional product attributes and did not want to pay for something that was not known to them (Johansson 1997).

Finally, being close to the market allows a company to enter the market first—or to be first to take advantage of a new opportunity. Having the advantage of being the first mover in a market can be substantial. First movers in markets benefit from getting established early and creating a positive connection with the market quickly. In fact, first movers may preempt future competition as well. This is a special benefit of size that results in profitability.

PARTICIPATION IN JOINT ACTIVITY

Global giants stay in the core markets of the industrialized world and exercise their market power by extending the existing product line, establishing pricing policies, and advertising, and using their own direct distribution channels. This is the most typical marketing strategy used by these companies and is the first of the five strategic alternatives presented in Figure 2-2. It is the easiest, the least costly, and the most convenient alternative. Global giants use it through their market power. The more common this strategy is, the more the majority in the world is forgotten. Large companies do not bother to adapt their marketing or product strategies according to market needs unless there is an undeniable critical mass in the market which is not often likely.

A person can buy IBM PCs on the same terms anywhere in the world. Using the second strategy shown in Figure 2-2, some global firms have entered secondary world markets, expecting

Figure 2-2. Global Marketing Strategies

	Strategic Option	Meaning
1.	Product and marketing practice extension	Using the same strategies everywhere
2.	Product extension marketing adaptation	While using the same products everywhere, using marketing strategies according to local market characteristic
3.	Product adaptation marketing extension	While using the same marketing strategies, adapting the product offering according to market needs
4.	Dual adaptation	Adjusting the product and the marketing strategies according to market needs
5.	Product and market invention	Innovating a new product and developing a new marketing strategy for it in each market

Source: Adapted and revised from Keegan (1999).

a critical mass to emerge. However, it is not profitable for a global giant to develop a new product or to go after a marginal market. Pillsbury entered some of the largest markets in India, but lost quite a bit of money because of this venture. It is not even economical for global firms to adapt their marketing activity when they are using the same products. Even if the products are changed to accommodate local needs and the company uses the same marketing strategies it uses elsewhere in the world, as illustrated by the third strategy, the overall activity is not likely to be successful. Secondary and tertiary third-world markets require not only the adjustment of the products, but also the adjustment of marketing strategies.

Strategies 4 and 5 in Figure 2-2 are such that global giants do not become involved unless the markets are sizable, which they aren't in third-world countries. Thus, Strategies 1, 2, and 3 are out of the question for Third World countries. Since those strategies are not applicable to these countries, they are not discussed. Strategy 4 is critical. A small company may be able to adjust its products and marketing activity to enter third-world markets easily and be successful. A small bicycle manufacturer, for instance, changes its product, making it sturdier, so the company can enter, say, a region of Pakistan. The company then adjusts its marketing strategies further to accommodate this market's values, needs, and behavior patterns.

Strategy 5 is another story. In essence, marketing to the forgotten majority takes some variation of this strategy. In this case, invention does not mean an earth-shaking development; it means a product that is simpler, less complicated, and cost and fuel efficient and that has a long life expectancy. Marketing invention means participating in a joint activity with a local firm that has local outreach.

Finding such a partner is not an easy task. (This concept is discussed further in Chapter 4.) However, if there is no partnership, there is no possibility of reaching the forgotten majority. After all, the small or medium international (or international wanna-be) company does not have the resources or the know-how to develop a direct marketing channel anytime soon. Finding a partner or partners is not enough. Being able to work with that partner is a critical activity; it requires sensitivity, understanding, respect, and communication. Sensitivity means that if the proposed activity were not mutually beneficial, it would be rather difficult to get cooperation from the partner. Culturally, businesses in different countries have different values and behavior patterns. If a small Western firm does not understand what makes a prospective partner tick, collaboration is impossible. Respect requires a company not think that a prospective partner should be just like it is or behave in a certain way. In other words, the company must have respect for what a partner does and is capable of doing. Sensitivity, understanding and respect cannot occur unless effective two-way communication takes place. The small Western business must realize that literal translation of the spoken word is not enough; literal translations can easily hide the true meaning of the conversation.

Third-world countries are conglomerations of hundreds and thousands of local markets that may be considered submarginal by global giants. Because of large companies' high costs and rather rigid patterns of doing business, they cannot function profitably in these markets. Therefore, they stay away.

However, a small entrepreneurial exporting or international company from the industrialized West can do very well in these markets. Such a firm does well by establishing a partnership with a local firm that shares the same goals and has similar entrepreneurial characteristics.

Some 50 years ago a small Swiss company went to Turkey to introduce the basics of modern supermarket principles to a few Turkish stores. The stores belonged to the Swiss company's Turkish partner. Some 50 years later, Migros, a large retail chain, is doing well with its Turkish partner. The company introduced four layers of grocery and basic consumer need supply stores in the existing four tiers of Turkish consumer markets. The same Swiss company has been expanding into Kazakhstan, Russia, and Bulgaria, using different names and working with local partners. If the entrepreneurial attitude did not prevail some 50 years ago, this company would not have achieved all the success it is enjoying now.

Partnership that is successfully functioning in one market can be expanded into a network. In a network, a partnership expands into other parts of a country and perhaps into neighboring countries, but the partnership may be expanding into related industries as well. In other words, networks can be an expansion of a partnership into other local markets or other related industries. As was mentioned earlier, the canned food processor from Florida may enter one part of central Africa and function well in collaboration with a local partner. The partnership may expand into a network as other partners are solicited and found in adjacent regions or countries. Similarly, the partnership may expand into other types of food marketing and distribution activities, such as meats or fresh fruits and vegetables. Thus, the partnership expands into a network in different directions. The canned food processor from Florida must be able to work successfully with the network it created or local efforts created. In either case, the canned food processor probably maintains formal or informal leadership of the network.

Of course, the network developed around the food processor from Florida may not be the only network. The food-processing network may be able to work with other supporting networks. For instance, the food-processing network may connect with a transportation network or with a refrigeration network. Such networks may be able to emerge and support each other. If the cooperation within the network is synergistic, the participants in the networks benefit, as do the regions or the countries where these networks function.

When multiple networks in one region or in one country find multiple networks in other countries, trading blocs may emerge. The food bloc that emerged because of the efforts of the food processor from Florida may connect with, say, a home appliances bloc from another country. Or the connection may be with another apparel network. Thus, trading blocs dealing with the forgotten majority take place, become functional, and expand. Trading blocs emerging between, say, Sri Lanka and Nepal are hardly any threat to Unilever, Nestles, or Procter & Gamble. These giants will continue to ignore the regional or local submarginal markets since they do not have adequate volume. The expansion process described here is a solution to the globalization activity that leaves most markets behind. The second wave of globalization may very well be the starting point of narrowing gaps between the haves and have-nots in the world. Small- and medium-size businesses can perform these all-important and much-needed functions if there is some encouragement from local and national governments as well as from the world's financial communities, such as the International Monetary Fund (IMF), the World Trade Organization (WTO), the World Bank, and others.

SUMMARY

The forgotten majority is not being served by global giants; therefore, the job of catering to these people is up to small- and medium-size companies. These firms can contribute to the well-being of the world's submarginal markets quite ably because they are innovative, are flexible, are close to markets, and function in joint activity.

Their innovativeness is reflected by the emergence of new ideas, by exploration of new opportunities, by not being conventional, and by being internally cohesive.

Small- and medium-size companies are also flexible. They can make sudden changes, they can change their direction, and they can make dramatically different plans—all very quickly.

These companies are close to the market and, as such, understand it well. Moreover, they are sensitive to consumer needs and have a good understanding of how consumers behave in these markets.

Finally, these firms participate in joint activity. They find partners who help create networks and eventually become part of the trading blocs.

REFERENCES

Johansson, Johnny K. (1997). *Global Marketing.* Chicago: Irwin.

Keegan, Warren J. (1999). *Global Marketing Management.* Upper Saddle River, New Jersey: Prentice Hall

Prahalad, C. K. and Lieberthal, Kenneth (1998). "The End of Corporate Imperialism," *Harvard Business Review,* July – August, 68–80.

3

Market Behavior
and Consumer Needs

In the second wave of globalization, international marketers must be close to the market. This means also understanding consumer behavior in submarginal markets. Although a lot of research has been conducted in the United States about consumer behavior, there has been little, if any, reason or effort to attach consumer behavior to cultural background. However, this is not the case when dealing with the forgotten majority. Companies must understand the cultural overtones of consumer behavior patterns in emerging markets because cultural differences are rather dramatic in these markets. Within the United States, one may loosely take the position that cultural differences between Michiganders and Californians are not nearly as profound as cultural differences between Turks and Pakistanis. In the latter case, it is necessary to study the culture and project it into consumer behavior problems accordingly (Samli 1995). Understanding cultural differences helps a company understand consumer behaviors, thereby allowing he firm to predict consumers' purchase patterns.

In various attempts to study consumer behavior, the effort has been to identify the similarities in values, behaviors, and needs. Such efforts have propagated the "one-size-fits-all" orientation and corporate imperialism. When dealing with the forgotten majority, the differences, not the similarities, need to be understood. The forgotten majority is widely scattered and is represented by multitudinous cultures with different values, different behavior patterns, and different needs. The entrepreneurial strength of small and medium firms is their sensitivity to these differences since they do not advocate a "one-size-fits-all" philosophy, nor are they bound by it.

CULTURE AS A KEY DETERMINANT OF CONSUMER BEHAVIOR

Based on Levin's (1938) work formulating consumer behavior, Boone and Kurtz (1992) developed a formula depicting consumer behavior. Their conceptualization of consumer behavior is formulated as $B = F (I,P)$, where B, consumer behavior, is a function of the interaction of interpersonal determinants (I), such as various groups and culture, and personal determinants (P), such as attitudes, learning, and perception (Samli 1995). The formula implies that consumer behavior is composed of the individual's psychological makeup and other influences. Perhaps this explanation of consumer behavior in the United States emphasizes the individual psyche and other people's influences more than cultural differences. However, exploring cultural differences is considered more critical in explaining consumer behavior in international settings. In this sense, Wallace (1964) associated consumer behavior directly to culture.

WALLACE'S THEORY

According to Wallace, culture is the all-encompassing force that forms personality (MacGregor 1983). Personality is the key determinant of consumer behavior. Culture forms the personality, and personality determines the consumer behavior. Figure 3-1 illustrates Wallace's theory. If a company understands cultural differences, to a certain extent, it can predict consumer behavior, resulting in important information about how to market its products in a country. Thus, culture, in essence, is the critical factor that determines consumer behavior as well as explains it. According to Wallace, therefore, understanding cultures is critical to explain and compare consumer behavior in different countries or regions (Samli 1995).

How do behaviors in different cultures vary? By observing the significant difference in behavior that exists between cultures, it is possible to assess a culture's far-reaching impact on individual behavior patterns. Chung (1991) and Samli (1995) attempted to distinguish the key features of European and Asian cultures by contrasting them in terms of how individuals thought, made decisions, and behaved in these cultures. One more dimension is added here that deals with purchase patterns. Figure 3-2 attempts to distinguish these two cultures by contrasting them in terms of the four dimensions mentioned above. Of course, these are broad generalizations, but they indicate the cultural dimensions of consumer behavior. These dimensions become more pronounced and focused as we analyze local cultural nuances are analyzed.

The far-reaching impact of culture can be observed in Figure 3-2. This impact is detected in individuals' overall functioning, indicating culture has an all-encompassing influence on people as individuals and as consumers.

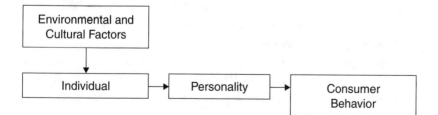

Figure 3-1. Role of Culture in Consumer Behavior
Source: Samli (1995).

Figure 3-2. A Comparison of European and Asian Cultures

European	Asian
MODES OF THINKING	
• Causal, functional	• Network, whole vision
• Linear, absolutely horizontal	• Nonlinear, relatively vertical
DECISION MAKING	
• To suit controls	• Based on trust
• Individual, free	• Group solidarity
• To suit the majority	• Reaching consensus
BEHAVIOR	
• True to principles	• To suit a situation
• Based on legal principles	• To suit a community
• Dynamic, facing conflict	• Harmonious, conservative
• Open, direct, self-confident	• Restrained, indirect withself-assurance
• Extrovert	• Introvert
PURCHASE PATTERNS	
• Individualistic	• Group influences
• Opportunistic	• Systematic
• Horizontal	• Vertical communication

Source: Adopted and revised from Chung (1991), Samli (1995).

By analyzing Figure 3-2, you can see that the Asian way of thinking is related to networking and deals with a broad and totalistic vision that connects the individual to society. Compared to the European view, the Asian way of thinking and behaving may not be so causally based on reasoning or so functionally based on actions; it is more vertically connected to some hierarchical order, such as the family or a reference group, and more connected to society as a whole.

With regard to decision making, whereas the individual is the focal point in Europe, group solidarity is considered the key factor in Asian cultures. Clearly, an individual's activity has limitations established by the group based on the well-being of the group itself.

Contrasting the behavior dimension shown in Figure 3-1, you can see that Asian cultures advocate coping with the situation as it occurs. Western cultures, on the other hand, advocate being true to principles. While the Western approach is challenging, direct, and confrontational, the Eastern approach is based on retaining harmony with the group and community. It is restrained and indirect.

Finally, Figure 3-2 briefly touches on purchase patterns. Although this topic and other components of Figure 3-2 are discussed in different parts of this book, it is important to point out that purchase patterns are connected to the other three components presented in the figure. As you can see, whereas purchase activity in Europe is individualistic, in Asia, group influences are critical. In European and North American culture, consumers seek opportunities on their own. In Asian cultures, as part of group influence, consumers go for tried and satisfactory products. Finally, whereas in European cultures individuals create or receive communication according to their choices, in Asian cultures, more vertical communication comes from family elders or the group.

The two extremes depicted in Figure 3-2 only illustrate differences. The culture may go in the direction presented, but never quite reach the extreme. Furthermore, although cultures change rather slowly, in time, the two extremes discussed in Figure 3-2 may converge. After discussion about the importance of culture in analyzing consumer behavior, it is critical that you have a general look at how cultures are identified.

IDENTIFYING CULTURES

Four key efforts (by Riesman, Hall, Hofstede, and Brislin) have been used to classify cultures. Refer to Samli (1995) for a detailed account of the discussion presented here.

Figure 3-3 provides basic information about the works and theories of these four scholars. Riesman (1953), primarily dealing with American society, classifies cultures into three categories: inner-directed, other-directed, and tradition-directed. Whereas inner-directed persons "internalize adult authority," other-directed persons are influenced by peers or contemporaries. Tradition-directed implies that people are guided by traditions (Samli 1995).

Hall (1976) proposes the high-context versus low-context dichotomy. In a low-context culture, messages are carried by words and messages are explicit. In high-context cultures, on the other hand, the emphasis is on the context of culture, such as background, interpersonal relations, and basic values.

Figure 3-3. Classification of Cultures

Scholar	Classification	Implications	Consumer Behavior
Riesman	Inner-directed Other-directed Tradition-directed	Some cultures are based on traditions, some on individualism, and some on others' influences	Where consumers get information and how they are influenced
Hall	High-context Low-context	Less information is transmitted as more emphasis is put on context of communication; in low-context, the emphasis is on more information and less emphasis on the context	How the communication in societies move and is shared
Hofstede	Classification of cultures based on collectivism, power distance, uncertain-avoidance, and masculinity-femininity.	It is important to analyze and group cultures that classify	Some cultures are very similar; others are very different.
Brislin	Individualistic Collectivistic	In some cultures, individuals are left alone; in others, individuals' lives have meaning only in a group	In some cultures, businesses must emphasize individuals; in others, they must emphasize group

Messages in such cultures are more implicit. As a result, less information is contained in verbal and written communications.

Hofstede (1983) used four different criteria to categorize cultures: individualism-collectivism, power distance, uncertainty avoidance, and masculinity-femininity. In an individualistic society, people look after their own interests. They are rather independent. In a collectivistic society, people identify with and behave by the values of their groups.

Power distance refers to the way a society deals with inequalities among people. The gap between the rich and the poor as well as the existing power structure within the society form behavior patterns and values.

Uncertainty avoidance implies that in some cultures, people are trained to take risk rather easily. People in such societies are more tolerant of different behavior and opinions. Other societies train their people to beat the future. People in these cultures are more nervous, emotional, and aggressive.

The masculinity-femininity spectrum deals primarily with the roles attributed to sexes. While men and women in some cultures perform various tasks and there is not much difference between the roles attributed to the sexes, in other societies, a sharp division exists between what men and women should do.

If a company understands a culture in terms of these four dimensions, we can predict consumer behaviors. This is not an easy task, but it is important for success in smaller markets.

Brislin (1993) and his associates singled out collectivism and individualism as the focus of their analysis. In an individualistic society, people focus their attention on their own goals and activities. On the other hand, a collectivistic society calls for emphasizing or paying attention to the goals of others when setting one's own goals (Samli 1995). Brislin's orientation is such that power distance, uncertainty avoidance and masculinity-femininity dimensions go primarily with individualistic-collectivistic dichotomy. By studying the latter, much can be accomplished.

Because it is easier to apply and to generalize, Brislin's collectivistic-individualistic dichotomy is used to explore consumer behavior that is attributable to the forgotten majority.

However, the high-context/low-context dichotomy is also referred to at certain points throughout the book because of its practical details in analyzing consumer behaviors.

INDIVIDUALISM VERSUS COLLECTIVISM

Individualism involves a special emphasis on one's own goals, with less attention to how these goals relate to those of others (except for immediate members of the nucleus family). In the workplace, for instance, people want to be recognized as hard workers or productive individuals based on their own merits rather than being considered merely good team players (Samli 1995).

Collectivism, on the other hand, emphasizes paying attention to the goals of others when setting one's own goals. These other influences can be a person's extended family or the organization where the individual works or social groups to which the individual belongs. In the workplace, individuals are satisfied if they are known as productive workers because they are members of groups that are recognized as productive, not only as good team players. But they receive self-identity through the group (Samli 1995).

Although Figure 3-2 shows, in part, the two different cultural patterns of European being individualistic and Asian being collectivistic, Figure 3-4 further explains the differences between the two. In individualistic societies, individuals are more likely to be left alone to solve their problems. In these societies, marketing efforts need to be directed to the individual. In collectivistic societies, the group is the key problem solver. In such cases, marketing efforts need to be directed to the opinion leaders of such groups.

If emotions are from within, which is the case in the individualistic society, individuals recognize the need for a product or service. By contrast, in collectivistic societies, emotions emanate from without. In this case, individuals are told they need certain products or services.

Figure 3-4. Individualism versus Collectivism

Individualism	Collectivism
Individual solves the problem himself or herself	Group solves the problem
Emotions are from within	Emotions are from without
Learning from one's own experiences is critical	Learning from others' experiences is critical
Elderly is not important	Elderly is important
Primarily short-term relationships	Long-term relations are prevalent
Cognitive influences are predominant	Affective influences are predominant

Source: Adapted and revised from Samli (1995).

In an individualistic society, individuals learn through their own experiences and efforts. From a marketing perspective, consumers should be contacted in such a way that they can gather the information, search for the product, and buy it.

In a collectivistic society, individuals learn from others' experiences. In such cases, marketers should appeal to the special experiences of the opinion leaders of groups, who, in turn, will influence the thinking of the group members.

The status of the elderly is different in these two cultures. In an individualistic society, the elderly do not have much status. However, in collectivistic cultures, the elderly are important. In collectivistic societies, marketing should make a special attempt to appeal to the elderly because they are, at least partially, opinion leaders. Furthermore, in collectivistic societies, prevalent in third-world countries, extended families are the rule. Many related people live under the same roof. In such cases, family elders usually make critical purchase decisions that will influence everyone in the group.

Members of individualistic societies experience widespread short-term relationships since individuals are rather independent and solve their own problems. Communicating with individuals in these societies is achieved on an individual basis. Mass media, for instance, provides enough information for individuals to make up their own minds. Individuals' short-term relationships can be identified and used as they change. On the other end of the spectrum, in collectivistic societies, long-term relationships and group belongingness are critical. Advertising efforts about products and services should be geared to the elderly or other opinion leaders so consumers can be persuaded (Samli 1995).

Consumer behavior is a display of preferences. The critical question is how these preferences are acquired and how they change. To understand the forgotten majority and cater to its needs, a company must explore this question carefully.

Understanding cognitive and affective influences contribute to the understanding of how preferences are acquired and modified. Cognitive learning can be described as active and individualistic ways of seeking, receiving, and processing information. From this perspective, cognitive learning is more prevalent in individualistic or industrialized society than in collectivistic societies, where the forgotten majority lives.

Affective learning, on the other hand, involves a lot of cultural influence. In more traditional and collectivistic societies, people are influenced by affective forces that are instilled in the culture, such as traditions, moods, emotions, and affective personality characteristics (such as optimism). Such influences result in Koreans thinking snakes represent wisdom, Egyptian fathers not calling their daughters "my sunshine" because the sun is considered cruel, and Turks not trusting people with light-colored eyes.

A company must understand consumer behavior well so successful marketing can enhance consumer satisfaction, particularly in third-world markets. Consumer behavior becomes the key factor in studying prevailing behavior patterns. These behavior patterns must be translated into marketing action.

HALL'S CONSIDERATIONS

As mentioned earlier, Hall classified cultures as high-context and low-context. Most less developed countries are considered high-context. A few important features of Hall's high-context concept complements the collectivistic culture that has been discussed. Specific features of these two types of cultural analysis explain, in general terms, consumer behavior in these cultures and provide a very specific set of "must do" activities for international marketers.

Figure 3-5 identifies six key features of high-context cultures that are prevalent in the countries and cultures where the forgotten majority lives. In general terms, in high-context cultures, human interaction is most important. Consumers trust each other, and a handshake is more important than an attorney-prepared legal document. Consumers in high-context cultures are used to receiving instructions and taking orders because these societies represent strong hierarchical power structures. Being poor forces individuals to live in crowded quarters and in close proximity with others. Thus, people are used to interacting with other people. Time is not a critical factor. Everything has its own time. Things will happen in due time. Therefore, negotiations, discussions, and other interactive involvements take a lot of time. Time-efficient products do not carry a major

Figure 3-5. High-Context Cultures

Features	Implications
Emphasis is on human interaction and handshakes rather than legal documents	Consumers pay more attention to direct personal contact
Hierarchical organizations and centralized power structures exist	Individuals are used to receiving instructions and taking orders
People live in crowded quarters	Human interaction is typical and relied on
Time is not important and is wasted on all activities	Negotiations and prolonged interaction is normal
No negotiations take place until the parties know each other well	Reliance on familiarity is critical
Sincerity, not legality, makes thing happen	Individuals' interaction with familiar people in familiar settings create more business

Source: Adapted and revised from Samli (1995).

appeal. Reliance on familiarity is strong, so much so that people do not do business with unfamiliar people. Quite closely related to familiarity is sincerity. Sincerity stresses a handshake is more powerful than legalized procedures.

Putting Two Key Cultural Traits Together

Whereas collectivistic cultures and their emphasis on affective learning deals with the marketing process in general, emphasis on high-context deals with the specific mechanics of marketing in third-world countries. Marketing practitioners who are interested in the forgotten majority must understand affective influences and high-context implications, which provide a valuable foundation for companies wanting to put together a successful marketing strategy in third-world countries. Figure 3-6 illustrates the combined marketing strategy implications of these two sets of cultural traits.

Four affective influences are cited. Cultural values are unique and individuals adopt those without thinking. Affective influences dwell upon emotional issues and events instead of facts and information. Affective influences are typically composed of opinion leaders' points of view. Finally, traditions that prevail in a country reflect a good portion of these affective influences.

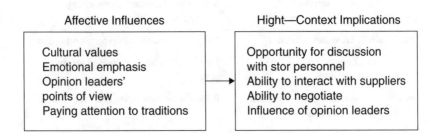

Affective Influences | Hight—Context Implications

Cultural values
Emotional emphasis
Opinion leaders'
points of view
Paying attention to traditions

Opportunity for discussion
with stor personnel
Ability to interact with suppliers
Ability to negotiate
Influence of opinion leaders

Figure 3-6. Marketing Strategy Implications

The high-context portion of Figure 3-6 deals with more practical aspects of the marketing plan. High-context implications emphasize human interaction; consumers are more comfortable because they have the opportunity to talk to somebody in a store or place of business. The ability to interact with suppliers gives an individual more confidence. Interaction also leads in the direction of negotiation, which is a favorite pastime in high-context cultures because time is not important. Finally, in high-context societies, opinion leaders play a critical role in what is purchased. In all negotiations, a handshake is more important than a contract.

Based on these observations, marketing strategies in third-world countries should concentrate, at the very least, on the following:

- Cultural values should not be ignored or forgotten in communications. Understanding cultural values and working with them is essential for success.
- Advertising, product characteristics, and company-related messages should not go against traditions. Countertraditional messages and products must be presented cautiously and slowly.
- Emotional messages should be geared more to opinion leaders and elders. When opinion leaders are moved, then advise others to follow certain instructions regarding purchases.
- Product or brand changes, if any, must take place gradually. Sudden changes do not play out well.
- Storekeepers must be close to consumers, provide good advice, and try to establish long-lasting relationships. Working with storekeepers is essential in getting a message across.
- Customers should be able to negotiate price, quality service, and other aspects of a prospective transaction. Human interaction presents itself strongly in negotiation processes.
- Storekeepers should attempt to communicate with elders and other opinion leaders. Similarly, elders and opinion

leaders should establish contact with storekeepers so they can be kept informed about products.

SUMMARY

This chapter presents a discussion of culture and its impact on consumer behavior in third-world countries. Wallace's theory states that cultural influences develop and modify personality which, in turn, dictates consumer behavior.

European and Asian behavior patterns differ with regard to modes of thinking, decision making, behavior, and purchase patterns. Four key efforts by Riesman, Hall, Hofstede, and Brislin have been used to classify cultures. Brislin and his associates focused their analysis on collectivism and individualism. In individualism, the emphasis is on the individual; in collectivism, the group is critical. Hall's high-context versus low-context dichotomy is used to supplement Brislin's approach. By combining the two, general features of marketing strategies can be identified. In collectivistic cultures, where the forgotten majority lives, affective, not cognitive, influences are critical, including emotionalism, cultural values, opinion leaders' influence, and traditions. In high-context cultures, individual interaction, ability to negotiate, close contact with store personnel, and influences of opinion leaders are critical aspects of purchasing behavior. Without understanding and accommodating the local culture, a company cannot succeed. A company's marketing strategy must be consistent with the local culture and resultant buying behaviors. Seven principles are necessary when marketing to the forgotten majority.

REFERENCES

Boone, Louis E. and Kurtz, David L. (1992). *Contemporary Marketing.* Fort Worth, Texas: The Dryden Press.

Brislin, Richard W. (1993). "Understanding Cultural Differences For Management on International Assignments," a seminar delivered at the University of Hawaii, June 24, 1993.

Chung, Tzol Zae (1991). "Culture: A Key to Management Communication Between the Asian-Pacific Area and Europe," *European Management Journal*, December, 419-424.

Hall, Edward T. (1976). *Beyond Culture*. Garden City, New York: Anchor Press/Doubleday.

Hofstede, Geert (1983). "The Cultural Relativity of Organizational Practices and Theories," Journal of International Business Studies, Fall, 75-89.

Riesman, David (1953). *The Lonely Crowd*. New York: Doubleday Anchor.

Samli, A. Coskun (1995). *International Consumer Behavior*. Westport, Connecticut: Quorum Books.

MacGregor, Robert M. (1983). "Wallace's Theory of Culture and Personality: A Useful Guide to Understanding Persons' Behavior," *Managing the International Marketing Function*, edited by Erdener Kaynak. Miami: Academy of Marketing Science.

Wallace, A. F. C. (1964). *Culture and Personality*. New York: Random House.

4

Negotiations
and Segments

Chapter 3 discussed how consumer behavior, particularly in third-world countries (where the forgotten majority lives), is strongly related to cultural background. In addition to understanding the key differences among these cultural patterns and the resulting differences in consumer behavior, a company must learn how to negotiate in these cultures. Also, markets should be segmented on the basis of cultural differences and behavior patterns. A Western company that is aiming at the forgotten majority must be sensitive to behavior variations and market segments. If the company does not understand the characteristics and uniqueness of market segments, it has no chance of establishing let alone sustaining, a presence. Since the process begins with negotiation, a company must develop appropriate skills in this area in order to enter and survive in third-world markets.

THE DIRECTION OF ATTENTION

Before a company gets into negotiation and segmentation, which are two key topics discussed later, it must identify the part of the world in which it is interested. Just how does a company find the regions, areas, or localities it hopes to enter? At least five separate approaches can be used for this purpose: trade statistics, the International Chamber of Commerce, Internet sources and trade announcements, logical deductions, and general mass media news.

Trade statistics show in which parts of the world trade is picking up and in which product and service categories. If trade is increasing for primary markets, secondary and tertiary markets may also be growing, thereby becoming better targets. However, as discussed later in this chapter, the opposite can be used to identify targets. The most forgotten markets are those markets trading the least, and a company may choose to concentrate on them.

The U. S. International Chamber of Commerce works with different countries and may have specific recommendations. These recommendations include specific geographic areas, as well as special names and product categories in an area.

Internet sources and trade announcements provide companies in certain parts of the world who are looking for partners. These leads can be fruitful if followed carefully. Internet leads are less likely unless the Chamber of Commerce of a country is attempting to become a matchmaker. Trade announcements are available in U.S. Department of Commerce publications.

Logical deductions imply analyzing the world and deriving certain conclusions by reasoning. For instance, countries developing their tourism can show a significant emergence in their secondary and tertiary markets. Therefore, the used-motorcycle market may be growing in southern Italy and certain parts of India.

Finally, general mass media news may indicate emerging desirable areas. For instance, no doubt, in a few years, there will be substantial economic aid to Afghanistan, accelerating the emergence of its markets for a large variety of goods and services.

NEGOTIATION SKILLS

Prospective Western exporters and partners in third-world markets must develop strong negotiation skills. As cultural features indicated earlier, consumers as well as businesses opt to negotiate rather that simply agree.

Negotiating with people in a collectivistic society, who are influenced by affective (emotional and cultural) factors and who receive high-context cultural influences, is much different that interacting with people from an individualistic society, who are influenced by cognitive (informational) factors and receive low-context cultural influences through written documents and general informational advertising.

The forgotten majority presides predominately in collectivistic cultures, is influenced by affective factors, and receives high-context cultural influences, perhaps through elders, opinion leaders, and storekeepers. The discussion that follows concentrates primarily on negotiating in collectivistic cultures.

NEGOTIATION IN COLLECTIVISTIC CULTURES

Figure 4-1 illustrates some key aspects of negotiations that take place in collectivistic societies. The negotiations revolve around affective influences. Typically, appeals are directed to emotions. Thus, emotion adds to the level of excitement that relates to the prospects of the outcome of the negotiation. If a conflict occurs, the arguments revolves around subjective feelings rather than cold and calculated reasoning. This situation is more palatable, as human interaction is highly valued in these societies.

There may be concessions. Give-and-take is the gist of the bargaining process and is widespread. Making concessions among others shows that a party is dealing with a worthy opponent. A display of appreciation can be the most important

Figure 4-1. Negotiation in Collective Settings

Negotiation Features	Negotiation Mechanics	Negotiation Outcomes
Negotiation style	Affective: Appeals made to emotions	Becoming excited about the prospects
Dealing with conflict	Opponent's arguments counteracted with subjective feelings	Creating an aura of "humanness" to come to a successful close
Making concessions	Give and take is a part of bargaining process	Showing that the other party is a worthy opponent
Opponent's concessions	Must be reciprocated	Acknowledging the sacrifice the other party is making
Starting position	Extreme	Creating the opportunity to meet in middle ground
Deadline	Not very important	Stating that the other party's time preference is suitable

Source: Adapted and revised from Samli and Hill (1998).

feature of the negotiation process. Positive expressions of what is happening and faith in the other party's ability to resolve the issue are critical.

If an opponent is making concessions, those concessions need to be reciprocated. In this way, the sacrifice the other party is making is acknowledged. Matching or exceeding the other party's sacrifice shows goodwill and the intention to do business.

Negotiations typically begin with each party holding opposite views. Extreme positions lead to a meeting in the middle—hence, the opportunity for more give-and-take, which is appreciated.

Collectivistic cultures are also high-context in nature. In high-context cultures, the time concept is not monochronic; it is polychronic, meaning everything will be handled in due time and there is no strict deadline. From a negotiation perspective, indicating that the other party's time frame is suitable is showing goodwill and appreciation for his or her preferences (Samli 1995). Since negotiations are likely to take place rather often, the ability to sharpen one's negotiation skills is very useful.

IMPLICATIONS FOR SEGMENTATION

You know that world markets are not homogeneous and that global giants do not concentrate on parts of the world that are not extremely lucrative. Large corporations know the lucrative segments of the world market, and they concentrate on these. This is why the concept of the forgotten majority becomes so critical. Third-world markets are composed of a myriad of small markets, which are all different and all ignored by global giants. But third-world markets present major opportunities for small firms. Since these markets are forgotten or ignored because they are not worthwhile for giant international firms to enter, they are wide open markets. They may be segmented in ways that are meaningful for small and intermediate size firms who are contemplating entering these marginal markets. At least two concepts are useful in segmenting the world's poorer markets: level of being forgotten and level of economic viability.

LEVEL OF BEING FORGOTTEN

This concept states that the more forgotten something is, the more attractive it can be. If the market segment or niche is totally forgotten, nobody is trying to enter that market and, hence, a small firm does not have much international competition trying to capitalize on existing opportunities. There are no perfect measures of levels of being forgotten, but the outskirts of Bombay, India, versus the outskirts of Kabul, Afghanistan, are not at the same level of being forgotten or not being known.

But being "off the beaten path" is not all that is involved. Some potential market segments show a higher degree of viability than others. Thus, viability is the second criterion used to identify possible international market segments that may become target markets. Some forgotten part of the world may have a certain type of viability that is important to know about. Consider, for instance, southeastern Turkey. An underdeveloped region of that country is being developed by a huge hydroelectric dam project, which is estimated to create jobs for 10 million people. Therefore, this region becomes viable. If projected economic development appears to be accurate this forgotten but viable region can become a strong target market for companies dealing with low-cost housing, economical generic pharmaceuticals, and other products or services. Certain viable markets in central Africa are in need of cooling systems, refrigerated warehousing, canned foods, and the like. Many parts of Vietnam need live cattle and other food-related resources. Although these markets are forgotten, they are viable and their needs must be addressed.

Figure 4-2 illustrates the way of thinking with regard to establishing such target markets. The upper left quadrant in the figure represents the most attractive portions of the forgotten majority market segments. Although the upper right quadrant is also a good market, many competitors, including some large companies, may be watching the market. Unless this market proves to be viable, it may not be attractive enough to consider. Special circumstances can make the lower left quadrant somewhat attractive. Cost savings because of economies of scale and logistics and proximity to other markets can make these segments attractive enough to consider.

	Most	Least
High Viability	Most attractive segments; the best prospects for entry	Although a good market, it is being watched by big competitors
Low Viability	A possibility if logistically and economically feasible	Not a good prospect since many others also have it in mind

Level of Economic Viability

Figure 4-2. Segmentation Considerations
Levels of Being forgotten

An ideal market segment has at least five features. It must be identifiable, measurable, significant, accessible, and actionable. Obviously, in order to target a market, the market must be identified and measured. If, for instance, the southeastern area of Turkey can be identified and, based on the viability factor, can be measured, a target market may be identified. Naturally, that target needs to be significant enough to make money.

The upper left quadrant of Figure 4-2 is considered to have these features (identifiable, measurable, and significant). However, accessibility and action require additional analysis. The potential target segment may be identifiable, measurable, and significant but may not be accessible. Accessibility of a target depends on at least three factors:

- Ease of entry
- Ability to find a local partner
- Threats of prospective competition

Ease of entry has many facets. Local and national laws and related restrictions are the foremost considerations. In some countries, the local or national government may provide a business with some assurance that it will not have competition for a while. This situation gives a company a head start, which can help in getting established in a market.

The ability to a find local partner or partners is critical in terms of gaining access to a market. Whether an undertaking will be a joint venture, a simple partnership, another type of strategic alliance (Samli and Hill, 1998) depends on the specific conditions of the agreement as well as the uniqueness of the local conditions. If a small manufacturing establishment decides to enter southeast Turkey and develop a joint venture with a local firm, major government concessions may be available regarding taxes, acquisition of land, and so on. Most international marketing books present more in-depth discussion on the pros and cons of different entry strategies. (See, for example, Samli and Hill 1998.)

Accessibility is closely related to how keen the existing competition might be. If a small firm is considering entering central

Figure 4-3. Possible Contrast Between Extremes

	Viable Forgotten	Not Viable/ Not Forgotten	Implications*
Identifiable	+	+	No Difference
Measurable	+	+	No Difference
Significant Difference	+	—	Significant
Accessible Difference	+	—	Significant
Actionable Difference	+	—	Significant

*Although Viable Forgotten and Not Viable/Not Forgotten can be identified and measured, in terms of significance, accessibility, and actionability, there must be significant differences between the two extremes in favor of being Viable Forgotten to support a decision to enter the market.

African markets but learns that a couple of global giants have been inquiring about the conditions and have concrete plans for entering these markets, accessibility cannot be considered positive for the small firm, since it cannot and would not want to compete with the global giants.

Finally, the target market must be actionable, meaning that a company's core competency areas are appropriate for a particular market. If a small business's core competency area is refrigeration, including institutional refrigeration, and that is the produce needed in the forgotten central African markets, then the action ability of the proposed target would be evaluated rather highly. Figure 4-3 illustrates that while both desirable and undesirable markets are identifiable and measurable, only the desirable markets are significant, accessible, and actionable for a firm to be successful.

MEASURING MARKET SEGMENTS

No matter how small or big a firm is, it must to attempt to approximate the size of the prospective target market. If the market were the whole country, obviously, the totals would imply the total national market. But if the market is a small region, the proportionate breakdown of the national total can be considered. If, for instance, the total national potential for refrigeration is X but only $1/10$ of the national market in terms of total population is the target market, then the approximate market potential for a product is X over 10 ($\frac{X}{10}$).

Figure 4-4 presents four different approaches for assessing target market potential. Only a brief description is presented here. For more details, refer to a basic international marketing text. (See, for instance, Samli and Hill 1998.) The four approaches are multifactor analysis, coefficient of income sensitivity, trend analysis, and macrosurveys.

MULTIFACTOR ANALYSIS

A target market can be evaluated on the basis of U.S. standards. The prospective target market is compared to the U.S. market on the basis of economic development criteria, such as electricity consumed per capita, and a series of lifestyle criteria, such as TV sets or automobiles per capita. Establishing a quality index for a target market in terms of American Standards, such as the United States being 100 percent the target market, may have a quality index of 15 percent as a good indicator. This quality

Figure 4-4. Approached to Estimating Market Potentials

Technique	Method	Impact
Multifactor Analysis	Analyzing the target market potential by comparing it to the U.S. economy	A realistic assessment of the target market
Coefficient of Income Sensitivity	Evaluating the target market economy by detecting marginal changes and their implications	A good estimate of the expected changes in the target market
Trend Analysis	Looking at the performance of the target market, projecting into the future	A simple way of estimating the target market growth
Macrosurvey	Observing relative level of development of the target market to decide how ready it is for products	A crude method of determining the quality of the target market and its potential

index is multiplied by the population of the target market as a percent of that of the United States. Finally, the adjusted market potential figure is multiplied by the total sales volume of, say, refrigeration sales in the United States (Samli and Hill 1998; Samli 1995). For instance, if the quality of the target market is 15 percent and the population of the target market is 10 percent of that of the United States, the market potential is .15 × .10 = .015, or 1.5 percent of the U.S. market. If the refrigerator company sells 100,000 refrigerators in the United States, in the target market, it will sell 1,500 refrigerators.

COEFFICIENT OF INCOME SENSITIVITY

As income of a target market is estimated to change, the impact of this change is not homogeneous. A 1 percent change in income can mean a 27 percent increase in food items. It may also mean a 2 percent decline, say, in public transportation. By analyzing the sensitivity of income changes in a target market, a company can approximate the market potential and expected changes towards its product line.

TREND ANALYSIS

If a company has past information regarding a target market's income and/or consumption patterns, by using trend analysis, the company can project into the future. The target market potential and its expected changes also can be approximated by this method.

MACROSURVEY:

In countries or regions where no adequate data exists, a company can attempt to observe how advanced the communities are. Approximating the level of advancement of these communities can enable a company to decide if that market is ready for its products. A place of worship, a school, a downtown with multiple stores, and every fourth home having a TV antenna may indicate that a home appliances business has potential in this area. Macrosurvey criteria can be tied into just how much a community with a certain level of development can buy.

Other techniques are used to measure market segments, but they are not applicable to third-world markets. Hence, they are excluded from the discussion here. The four approaches discussed here may indicate whether a company should consider entering, for example, Pakistan, Turkey, or Central Africa. Once, say, three higher priority markets are identified, a decision has to be made by the company. Being a small company, it cannot cater to all of the markets that appear to be accessible and actionable.

The company needs to decide which of the markets analyzed is most appropriate to enter. To assess the appropriateness of the market, the company must ask the three questions that were raised earlier: (1) How easy is it to enter the market? (2) Do we have a reliable local partner to work with? (3) What is the potential for prospective competition? The answers to these questions are subjective criteria that are not the same in each potential market. Of all of the potential markets, the one (or ones) that appear to be more favorable in terms of these three questions is likely the preferred market.

Additional considerations about the products a company is planning to market must come into play. For instance, in collectivistic and high-context markets, a company must work with small local retailers, rather than self-service outlets, because storekeepers need to explain to the consumer how to use or take care of the product. Small enterprises, particularly store managers, are important in providing advice to consumers. Therefore, the availability of certain types of stores is an additional important consideration in selecting target markets to enter.

SUMMARY

Entering third-world markets requires mastery of the art of negotiation. In collectivistic cultures, human interaction and negotiation are critical.

The level of being forgotten is an important feature with regard to market segmentation. The more "off the beaten path" of international trade a proposed market is, the more likely it can be important for a business. The viability of a proposed target is also critical. If a target is likely to go through a major economic overhaul or if major economic projects are planned, the target market is viable. The more viable and more forgotten markets are important targets for small firms.

However, target markets must be identifiable, measurable, significant, accessible, and actionable. If all of those conditions are met, then a company must look at the size of the market. Four basic techniques are used to estimate market potentials: multifactor analysis, coefficient of income sensitivity, trend analysis, and macrosurveys. The size of the proposed market provides some indication about profitability and the possibility of expansion, and perhaps how fast a company must move to preempt future competition.

REFERENCES

Samli, A. Coskun and Hill, John R. (1998). Marketing Globally.
    Lincolnwood, Illinois: NTC Books.
Samli, A. Coskun (1995). International *Consumer Behavior*,
Westport, Connecticut: Quorum Books.

5

Partnering for Profit

I f a small Western company has any hope of entering third-world markets, it must find a partner and work closely with that partner. Having a strategic alliance or a partnership with a local firm is almost a necessity for a small Western firm wanting to cater to a market that reaches the forgotten majority. This is not a simple task. Most small and medium Western companies do not have the skills needed to search for and find a partner. However, without effective partnering, it is virtually impossible for them to enter third-world markets and be effective.

SOLICITING PARTNERS

For a company to be able to solicit the type of partner with whom it could work successfully, the company needs good understanding of what a prospective partner can expect; likewise, the partner must have a clear-cut vision as to whether the company can meet its needs.

Figure 5-1 illustrates the priorities of both parties and how, typically, priorities of both parties differ. These differences in priorities make it even more difficult for two parties to connect and create a meaningful relationship. The prospective partner must be an ongoing business that is reasonably successful; it must know the market well and perform even better. But then, not all successful ongoing businesses are open-minded or flexible enough to work with a foreign partner. There must be some evidence that the prospective partner is capable of working with a foreign firm.

It is important to assess:

- How ethnocentric a firm is.
- Whether it has any international experience.
- Why it is seeking an international partner.

These are critical issues for a party to explore before sharing a future with an unknown company.

If a potential partner is ethnocentric, it is probably not open to other cultures and other ways of thinking. If a prospective partner has not had any international experience, its ability to handle a partnership is questionable. Seeking an international partner can be a positive and a negative sign. A company showing ambition is a positive sign.

A prospective partner must have a preference for quality. A company's reputation in a market is closely connected to the prospective partner's quality, and the company's success in the market will be enhanced if that commitment to quality is on the rise. The small firm does not have an international reputa-

Figure 5-1. What's Expected of Partners

Priorities of a Firm Regarding a Partner	Priorities of a Prospective Partner
• Must be in the market and must be successful	• Some financial assets
• Must show some skills or evidence that it can work with a foreign partner	• Some unique competencies
• Must display a preference for quality	• Certain products and services that are not existing in the market
• Must have plans for expansion	• Ambitious plans for growth
• Must have a good reputation regarding reliability	• A competitive advantage that is suitable for the market

tion. Therefore, the partner's way of doing business will determine success or failure.

A prospective partner's level of ambition is a critical concern. In many traditional societies and third-world markets, businesses function, but lack ambition for growth. Expansion plans, even if they are unwritten and superficial, are a powerful clue to the worthiness of a prospective partner to work with and share a future in the market. Alliances based on the ambition of a partner's capabilities for growth are likely to be successful (Garrett and Dussage 2000). A prospective partner must fit with a company's ways of conducting business and must share its dreams in terms of performance and success in the market. By the same token, a company must be able to show that what it has in mind is in the realm of its capabilities and that combining its efforts with those of a prospective partner can generate synergistic reaction and benefit both parties.

A prospective partner must enjoy a good reputation for reliability in product and service. A company's reputation in a market is not developed, but is based on the reputation of its partner. But what does a prospective partner require (or at least wish for)?

THE PROSPECTIVE PARTNER'S EXPECTATIONS

Figure 5-1 points out some of the key expectations a prospective partner has in mind. Being in economically less developed or developing countries, a local partner expects some financial support up front. Perhaps more than that, a partner expects unique competencies, such as the skill to develop a desirable, but thus far unavailable, product. A company's unique competencies can entice a prospective partner in its direction.

Also, a company that can offer attractive products or services has an easy time finding a partner. A small refrigeration business will have no difficulty finding partners in central Africa if their products do not exist in the market but are in demand.

The ability to generate new products is an additional strength welcomed by a prospective partner.

If a Western company has ambitious plans and a prospective partner is made privy to those plans, the Western firm can have a rather easy time finding partners. These ambitious plans may include, among others, expanding in the market or jointly entering other markets.

A company's strengths and attractiveness as a prospective partner revolve around generating a suitable competitive advantage for itself as well as for a prospective partner. Creating, sharing, and sustaining a competitive advantage are closely related to functional arrangements.

As a company looks for a partner and as a prospective partner looks for a company, the priorities of the two parties are different, which both must keep in mind before entering a negotiation phase.

FUNCTIONAL ARRANGEMENTS

Although each case is different and has its own functional arrangements, Figure 5-2 illustrates basic arrangement areas. If, functionally, a company cannot generate a synergistic alliance, it is not likely to succeed.

At the outset of an alliance, the parameters of functional responsibilities must be established so no major conflicts come up later on. This means the two parties must have a good idea as to who does what.

More specifically, since the information is critical for the long-term success of an alliance, the parties must agree to how the image of the venture is to be developed and enhanced. This forces the two parties to think not only of the present but also of the future.

Early on, the parties must decide who is responsible for local distribution of the products of this alliance and how much expansion possibility exists. In fact, if the local partner does not

Figure 5-2. Functional Arrangements

Functions	Implications
Who does what	Establishing the functional parameters
How the image is developed and enhanced	Forcing both parties to think futuristically
Who makes decision for local distribution	Making sure the local partner is expanding
How the proceeds are shared	Planning in advance how gains are to be distributed
What the procedures are for expansion	Making sure expansion is taking place
What the control mechanisms are	Making sure that neither party is taking advantage of the other
How accounting procedures are established	Establishing an accounting system that is realistic and fair

have the capability to expand, the arrangement should not proceed any further.

How the proceeds are to be shared is a critical issue. The two parties must agree upon how to divide the profits and losses how to take profits, if any, out of the country. Different countries have different guidelines. Therefore, planning in advance how the gains will be distributed is a must, rather than a simple precautionary measure.

The functional arrangements are not permanent; they are likely to change for good reasons. Establishing a control mechanism generates flexibility for the arrangement. If the agreed-upon conditions are not satisfactory or if performance is stifled because of poorly made arrangements, having a control mechanism that indicates the problem and solves it equitably is critical. Such a control mechanism cannot be established suddenly and simply. Therefore, the parties should make sure that a previously established control system is in place and is working well (Samli 1985).

Most of the functional arrangements discussed here are directly or indirectly related to the accounting procedures established at the outset. Since an accounting system indicates the results of the parties' efforts, the more accurate the indicated results, the more realistic and fair the accounting system.

When dealing with future expansion, a company must explore the possibilities for expansion in the market where the partner is and other expansion arrangements into new markets.

ENTERING THE MARKET WHERE THE PARTNER IS

A company searches for a partner so it can enter a third-world market. Chances are that this is a niche market and is only one portion of the national market. Therefore, a company must decide whether to expand within that country or to enter other niche markets with the same partner or have a different partner in each niche market. There are pros and cons for both alternatives. A company must make a decision according to the conditions it is facing. However, particularly in high-context cultures, if a particular alternative preferred by a firm is not made clear to the local partner, the company's reputation and attempt to do further business in the market can be seriously jeopardized.

ENTERING NEW MARKETS JOINTLY

If a partnership works well, both parties may agree to enter another foreign market jointly. However, an entrepreneurial small firm will probably do better in another country with a partner from that country. A Turkish company specializing in various industrial textiles enters Iran with one local partner and Brazil with another partner.

In addition to having a successful partnership, which can be a strong incentive to continue as is and enter a new market jointly in a different country, other conditions may force the partnership to enter another market together. The Japanese, for instance, must partner with Turkish firms (another Moslem country) to enter Saudi Arabian markets.

Regardless of the type of arrangement that is agreed upon, the partners must share knowledge if their relationship is to be sustained. The parties involved must consider different conditions with regard to knowledge sharing.

KNOWLEDGE SHARING

Three key areas in knowledge sharing need to be considered: self-protection, joint benefit, and technology transfer. Self-protection is vital, particularly with regard to the sharing of trade secrets. Assume the refrigeration company is again considering entry into the central African market. What kind of self-protection issues may enter into the picture?

SELF-PROTECTION

What are some of the dangers? The partner can acquire information and technology and make a deal with another (say, American) company. Or the partner, after having mastered the technology, may go to another neighboring country alone. Similarly, within the same country, the partner may go to another niche market alone. Thus, there is a key question with regard to self-protection: Just how much knowledge can a company impart without being taken advantage of? The answer to this question must be considered in original negotiations. Again, each case depends on its own merits, but developing an aura of mutual confidence is the key to success.

JOINT BENEFIT

On the other end of the spectrum, a company must share knowledge with its partner. The more knowledgeable the partner is in production and marketing, the greater the chance of joint success. Thus, a company finds itself in a paradoxical situation; the company must give information so its partner can perform better, but the company reveals vital information that might jeopardize its position later on. The best solution to this problem is for the company to continue with research and development. If and when the partner masters the procedures and information and begins thinking about leaving, the company has new information that the partner does not possess. Of course, if the partnership grows stronger, there may be no need to keep the new knowledge from the partner. If the synergistic relationship is getting stronger, the partner is probably not thinking about leaving, abandoning the relationship. Regardless of the relationship and its strength, a company must continue with its own research agenda independently.

TECHNOLOGY TRANSFER

If the refrigeration company is going to produce components or finished products, it must have an appreciation of technology transfer and some of its key problems.

Technology transfer is a rather involved activity that has serious risks. Recall the Bhopal incident in India. The Union Carbide plant run by Indian nationals had a major explosion. About 2,000 people died and over 20,000 were wounded—all because the workers were not trained properly and were not aware of the risks. A partner must be capable of using the technology efficiently.

Figure 5-3 highlights the necessary capabilities a partner must have. In fact, the items may be used as a checklist if there is more than one prospective partner. Along with a scoring system, it would not be difficult to distinguish among a few candidates.

The figure illustrates that a prospective partner, in order to adopt the technology and use it effectively, must have technical capability. But without qualified (or at least trainable) personnel, technical capability is not enough. Furthermore, local supplies of raw materials, parts, and other necessities must be adequate and a prospective partner must have access to them. Having access to transportation can be critical, depending on the finished product. If the product requires special handling, the transportation system must be able to accommodate that requirement. If the product is to be distributed at great dis-

Figure 5-3. Partner's Abiloty to Receive the Technology

Required Capabilities	Expected Outcomes
Technical capability	Ability to use the technology
Qualified personnel	Efficient workers
Local supplies	Cost-efficient production
Access to transportation	Efficient deliveries
Quality control	Production of high-quality products
Ability to work with local authorities	Creation of positive conditions for the business
Safety cautiousness	Ability to handle somewhat dangerous procedures

tances, the transportation system must be able to accommodate that requirement too. Overall, a quality control system used for other activities gives some indication about whether the prospective partner could develop one for a joint product.

One of the most critical considerations is the partner's ability to deal with local authorities. Conditions are different from one place to another. A company cannot assume that dealings with local or regional regulators will be smooth-going with no problems. A small company cannot function without a local partner in the target market who knows how to deal with local authorities.

Finally, the partner-to-be must be cautious about potentially dangerous procedures. This feature is important when the product line contains sensitive products that may be dangerous to produce or consume.

The search for a partner becomes crucial if a company is determined to survive in a market.

IN SEARCH OF A PARTNER

From the discussion so far, you know that finding a suitable partner is a critical issue. In addition to a company having a clear understanding about what we expect from a good partner, the company must go through the mechanics of the search process. The search process is displayed in Figure 5-4. There are five major steps in the process of searching for and finding a partner.

Step 1 — Original Contact:

There are at least three sources of names from which a partner can be found. The Internet is perhaps the easiest and most practical way of generating names. The embassy of the country and perhaps the commercial attaché in the embassy can be helpful in suggesting some names. Finally, the chamber of commerce of the country is likely to be receptive and cooperative.

Step 2 — Communication:

Once a list is generated, a letter of intent should be sent to all candidates. However, simultaneously, some variation of the checklist presented in Figure 5-3 may be used to determine the most appropriate partner-to-be.

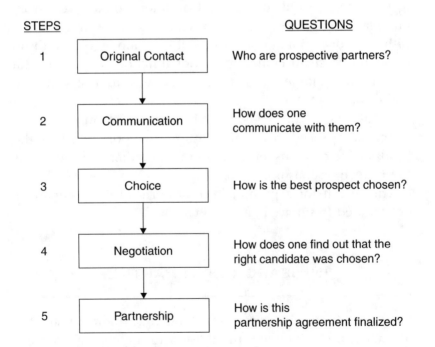

STEPS		QUESTIONS
1	Original Contact	Who are prospective partners?
2	Communication	How does one communicate with them?
3	Choice	How is the best prospect chosen?
4	Negotiation	How does one find out that the right candidate was chosen?
5	Partnership	How is this partnership agreement finalized?

Figure 5-4. Finding a Partner

Step 3 — Choice:

After step 2, the list may be reduced to two or three names. At this point, one name needs to be singled out. From the response to letters of intent and the results of the checklist analysis, a choice can be made.

Step 4 — Negotiation:

The ideal situation is to have personal interaction leading to face-to-face negotiation. Much of the discussion presented in Chapter 4 is appropriate at this stage of the process.

Step 5 — Partnership:

A decision with regard to partnership is the outcome of the first four steps. The result of such a decision, even if it is not detailed in a contractual agreement, is very difficult to terminate because of cultural provisions. Hence, a handshake must come at the end of carefully detailed production and marketing plans as part of a total strategy.

SUMMARY

Finding a partner is critical for a company's success in third-world markets. A company must contrast its priorities with a prospective partner's priorities to better understand the prospective partner's psyche. Establishing a functional working arrangement with a prospective partner is necessary. Seven key functions are identified: (1) who does what, (2) how the image is developed and enhanced, (3) who makes decisions for local distribution, (4) how the proceeds are shared, (5) what the procedures are for expansion, (6) what are the control mechanisms, and (7) how accounting procedures are established.

Another key issue is technology transfer. Particularly in technical and chemical products and where local production is considered, a partner's ability to adopt the technology and run it effectively is a major requirement. A prospective partner must have certain capabilities, without which the technology cannot be transferred successfully.

Finally, a company must conduct a search process to find a good partner. In the final analysis, if the search process is not adequate, the company may end up with an undesirable partner. Terminating a partnership is rather difficult, if not impossible.

REFERENCES

Garrett, Bernard and Dussage, Pierre (2000). "Alliances versus Acquisitions: Choosing The Right Option," *European Management Journal*, February, 63–69.

Samli, A. Coskun (1985). *Technology Transfer*, Westport, Connecticut: Greenwood Publishing.

6

Alliances, Strategic
or Otherwise

C hapter 5 discussed the need to have a partner in the target market and how to choose the partner and work on the partnership. However, partnering in a third-world market with a local counterpart does not say much about a higher set of considerations regarding a strategic alliance.

When connecting with a partner, the key issue in conventional thinking prevails: Is this partnership workable? Thus, the strategic part may not be examined. All alliances are not strategic; many are formed for convenience. Unless a company goes out of its way to strategize the alliance, it may remain just convenience. When Pillsbury entered the Indian market to sell wheat flour, the local partner was considered more of a convenient local support rather than a major strategic alliance. General Motors entered into a strategic alliance with Daewoo in South Korea, but it did not work. Many alliances do not work because the distinction between "convenience" and "strategic" are not carefully distinguished.

CONVENIENCE ALLIANCES

Although most alliances are called "strategic alliances," many of them are not strategic. They fulfill a need other than development and implementation of a strategy.

Convenience alliances are likely to achieve three separate goals. These goals are financial, entry specific, and globalization.

FINANCIAL

Convenience alliances typically are organized so the partner or partners can get financial help. Regardless of who has what and who gives how much, a convenience alliance to receive financial support is a far cry from a partnership to develop and implement a strategic posture. When entering third-world markets, prospective partners are likely to be highly motivated having this financial prospect; however, the alliance is not likely to work because it emphasizes the wrong feature.

ENTRY SPECIFIC

Convenience alliances are sometimes formed to enter a specific market. To enter the Saudi and Kuwait markets, the Japanese had to work with Turkish firms. The Turkish firms could enter these markets easily, whereas the Japanese would not have been able to do so. Thus, convenience alliances for the purpose of entering a market are functional, but still they are not strategic in the sense of developing a plan for creating competitive advantage and market power.

GLOBALIZATION

Many companies enter into convenience alliances so they can globalize. Establishing an international name and reputation through a series of convenience alliances has been a way to internationalize a firm. Many large firms have become global using such an approach. Two Korean firms, Emerson and Samsung, entered many alliances in order to globalize. The companies have been reasonably successful partly because they also had strategic plans. But again, this type of globalization is not necessarily a strategic move in terms of generating market power and competitive advantage (Samli and Hill 1998).

Although important, such convenience alliances play a totally different role than strategic alliances. As is discussed in the following section, a vast difference exists between strategic alliances and convenience alliances. For a small or medium Western company, convenience alliances are an exercise in futility. A company's goal is not just to enter a particular market; with a strategic alliance, the company can expect to generate a synergistic relationship with a local partner. Such a strategic alliance helps develop competitive advantage and market power, leading to success in a market.

STRATEGIC ALLIANCE

The synergistic nature of a relationship is the decisive factor in determining whether an alliance is strategic. The strategic nature of the alliance can be evaluated on the basis of risks it takes. Some authors divide these rules into two major groups, relational risks and performance risks (Das and Teng 1999).

A relational risk involves a lack of commitment from the partners. It shows itself through a lack of shared information, a lack of communication, a lack of attention to security in operations, and a lack of a control mechanism.

Performance risk is related to how likely an alliance is to fail because of internal and external factors the partners cannot control even if they try. The alliance fails internally because the parties are not competent, and the alliance fails externally because many factors are working against it, such as economic conditions and changing government policies.

Since not much can be done to change external adversities, the emphasis here is on internal performance synergy-related features. Figure 6-1 presents the key elements of synergism.

Figure 6-1. What's Expected of Partners

Relational Synergy	Expected Outcomes
Information Sharing	Both parties are informed
Communication	Information flows in both directions
Security	Both parties are trustworthy
Control	The total process is controlled by both parties

Performance Synergy	
Flexibility	Overall process becomes more adjustable
Productivity	Overall productivity goes up
Promotion	The joint organization is better promoted
Distribution	Neither party can succeed alone

When a small- or medium-size Western company is in the process of establishing a strategic alliance, there is not much room for alternatives. The synergistic characteristics of the alliance do not allow additional room for maneuvering. Particularly, performance synergy must be at its best. The operations of the alliance must be flexible enough for changing market conditions. The alliance must be productive. It must be able to promote itself in the local market. Equally important, the alliance must be capable of distributing its product or products in a particular market.

Synergism is the key word when it comes to a successful strategic alliance. The synergistic complementarity between the two partners is so critical that a question needs to be asked about the level of synergism: How can the parties be more synergistic? At the formation stage, the more carefully and in depth the alliance is analyzed, the greater the likelihood there is of a successful alliance being formed (Glaister and Buckley 1999).

Remember, all strategic alliances are partnerships, but all partnerships are not strategic alliances. In fact, some intended strategic alliances turn out to be unsuccessful because, in reality, they are not adequately strategic.

SCREENING PROCESS

For a strategic alliance to be synergistic, proactive, and successful, in-depth screening of the conditions of the proposed partnership are needed before it is formed. Figure 6-2 illustrates a seven-step process, going from general to specific.

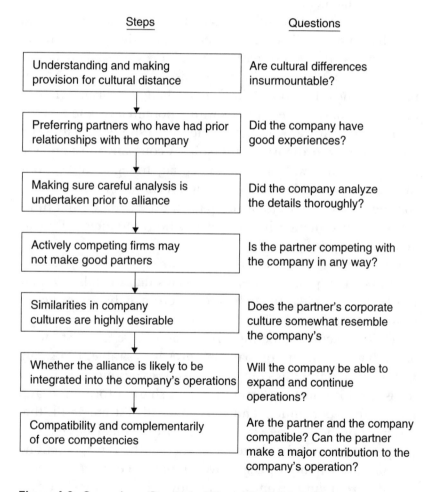

Steps	Questions
Understanding and making provision for cultural distance	Are cultural differences insurmountable?
Preferring partners who have had prior relationships with the company	Did the company have good experiences?
Making sure careful analysis is undertaken prior to alliance	Did the company analyze the details thoroughly?
Actively competing firms may not make good partners	Is the partner competing with the company in any way?
Similarities in company cultures are highly desirable	Does the partner's corporate culture somewhat resemble the company's
Whether the alliance is likely to be integrated into the company's operations	Will the company be able to expand and continue operations?
Compatibility and complementarily of core competencies	Are the partner and the company compatible? Can the partner make a major contribution to the company's operation?

Figure 6-2. Screening a Strategic Alliance Before It Is Formed

Source: Adapted and revised from Glaister and Buckley (1999).

The first step deals with a general but important analysis, cultural distance. Here the compatibility of the different cultures of the prospective alliance members is analyzed. A lot of cultural distance may exist between German company and a prospective partner in Nepal. Numerous U.S. firms have had difficulty dealing with Chinese and Korean partners. Understanding the cultural distance in advance and making provisions for it is a necessary condition for the formation of a strategic alliance.

If the partners in a strategic alliance know each other and have had previous dealings with each other, depending on the experiences from these earlier experiences, the alliance may be put together successfully. Since this is not a common occurrence, the next best possibility is to exchange information with others who have done business with a potential partner.

Finding a partner who helps synergize a strategic plan is different from an ordinary partnership. A company must analyze how the alliance will function and what strategic implications must be considered in advance, but not simply in terms of task sharing. Very specifically, a company must examine what functions would enhance its market position and help fulfill its goals.

If our strategic partner-to-be is an actively competing firm in the same area, past experience indicates that the alliance may not be a good idea. In such cases, there may be a conflict in viewpoints and a lack of cooperation.

While directly competing firms may not be good strategic allies, having similar company cultures is desirable. If a small, young, and ambitious company likes to experiment with new ideas, explore new opportunities, and share information and goals with its personnel, it must partner with a strategic ally that has most of those same corporate features. Similarities in company cultures lead the strategic alliance in the right direction.

From a company's perspective, the alliance must not be a very different entity from what already exists. On the contrary, the alliance must be integrated into the company's operations and strengthen them, particularly in the target market area.

This is particularly critical in terms of the future activities of the alliance. A strategic alliance may decide to go to an adjacent country where the market conditions are similar and where the alliance may find another partner to join the strategic alliance.

All of the above points (Figure 6-2) lead in the direction of the most important feature of the strategic alliance. First is compatibility between the ally and the company. If a company is extremely anxious and deliberately overlooks certain points of noncompatibility, it is likely to pay the price later on. If, for instance, the cultural distance is too wide, the company has not had positive dealings with the partner, the partner has been actively competing with the company, or the partner and the company have different management cultures, the two are not compatible.

The next alliance feature is complementarity. In strategic alliances, complementarity needs to be more than the matching of skills. The matched skills also need to be core competencies of both parties. Thus, the parties involved will put forth their best efforts. Each side needs that best effort from the other party for the alliance to be truly synergistic. Thus, synergism is the key word in a strategic alliance.

OTHER TYPES OF ALLIANCES

Earlier in this book, two other types of alliances were mentioned: home front alliance and target market alliance. Since entering third-world markets is hardly an ongoing plan of small- and medium-size Western firms, companies one or the other of need these two alliances just to get started. With regard to a home front alliance, a firm gains managerial (if needed) information and financial support. Simultaneously, the firm is put in touch with prospective partners and/or customers in the target market. Together, the home front alliance and target market alliance are not likely to be synergistic. They may not even be a convenience alliance, but the two can begin the process of going to an overseas market and making the conditions suitable for a future strategic alliance.

SUMMARY

For a small- or medium-size firm, entering a foreign market is not usually possible. Most small- and medium-size firms do not have international experience. And even if they did, they could not function without some type of partner.

All partnerships are not strategic alliances, but all strategic alliances are partnerships. There are three types of alliances. The first is a convenience alliance. If a company wants to enter a market, receive financial help, or become global quickly, it can use partners to fulfill these objectives.

The most important alliance is one that is strategic. Strategic alliances are synergistic. There are two types of synergy. Relational synergy is where two parties are very much in sync. Performance synergy occurs when two parties manage to function well, respectively, in their core competency areas.

Before a strategic alliance becomes a reality, it must be examined carefully using a seven-step screening process. A company has much to lose by not considering the questions in the screening process to become a strategic alliance.

The third type of alliance, also discussed in Chapter 1, is a supportive alliance. This is a combination of a home front alliance and a target market alliance. Since most small- and medium-size businesses are not internationally inclined, the home front alliance and target market alliance jointly provide direction, support, information, and other services a U.S. company needs to begin functioning in a third-world country.

Convenience alliances, strategic alliances, and supportive alliances all have critical roles to play.

REFERENCES

Das, T. K. and Teng, Bing-Sheng (1999). "Managing Risks in Strategic Alliances," *The Academy of Management Executive*, Nov., 50–62.

Glaister, Keith W. and Buckley, Peter J. (1999). "Performance Relationships in U.K. International Alliances," *Management International Review*, Second Quarter, 123–147.

Samli, A. Coskun and Hill, John R. (1998). *Marketing Globally*. Lincolnwood, Illinois: NTC Books.

7

Products and
Services Offering

The forgotten majority has many needs that are not satisfied. This does not mean, however, that these consumers buy any product or service even though they need it. Since money is scarce, consumers in third-world markets are rather particular. They want to know that the little money they have is not wasted. On the other hand, it is not very difficult for a company to establish itself and its brands in these markets if the products and services are well suited for the local needs. Because of scarcities, consumers in third-world markets think twice and are cautious before trying a new item. But once consumers are used to products and certain services, they remain loyal to them. If they are loyal to certain products and brands, they buy them almost automatically. In other words, in time, they get used to buying these products. In such cases, inertia plays an important role in the purchase of some products and services. A company might decide to encourage the emergence of such an inertia, but this is not easy to do.

Without having a product or service that is needed and/or wanted in a market, a company cannot hope to enter a third-world market and make progress. A company must deal with many considerations about its product offering. If a company wants its product produced in a target market by a partner or jointly, the technical characteristics of the product become a critical consideration.

HIGH TECH, LOW TECH, NO TECH

For high-tech products, a company must realize that a target market may not be able to produce this product. Most third-world countries emphasize labor-intensive, rather than capital-intensive, products and industries. For high-tech products the question is this: To what extent can the production process be manualized? Furthermore, is it worthwhile to manualize the process? Manualization lowers production costs, since labor is less costly in third-world countries. However, manualization may not be possible. In that case, the question is as follows: Can high-tech production of products be sustained in the target market? Additionally, certain requirements regarding raw materials, labor, energy, and other infrastructure-related issues must be carefully assessed.

As was discussed earlier, if a product is going to be produced in a target market, technology transfer is critical. It is possible to develop a modified technology suitable for the partner's capabilities and lower labor costs. However, if there is technology transfer, it must be done effectively and successfully. If a company is providing the technology, it must also provide control mechanisms to determine whether the technology is working satisfactorily.

Having, relatively speaking, low-tech (apparel, textiles, and automobiles) or even no-tech products (commodities, food supplements) makes it easy for a company to deal with a partner in a target market. If products are partially or fully produced in the target country, labor costs are low; therefore, products can be sold at lower prices.

The most critical issue after finding a partner and establishing a strategic alliance is identifying the product or service that is likely to make an impact in the market.

If, for instance, a medium-size bicycle manufacturer was considering going to rural Pakistan, the company might want to develop a product that functions well on dirt roads and carries three people or semibulky packages. These features could easily be incorporated into a series of prototypes.

Figure 7-1 lists some of the basic questions the bicycle manufacturer should answer before entering the rural Pakistani market. The first question is decisive in terms of whether the company should consider the target market as a possibility. A company may be able to adapt its product line to meet the needs of the market. For example, the bicycle manufacturer may be able to offer a variety of related products—from simple motorcycles to roller skates. In societies where there is no public transportation and not too many options in consumer mobility (rural areas), products offered by the bicycle manufacturer can be very useful.

The question is whether a company's products can be produced in the target market. A small bicycle manufacturer may be interested in simply exporting its finished products. But such a proposition implies a short-term arrangement. If a company continually exports to its target market, eventually the products will be pirated; the company may lose control of its marketing activities and witness the deterioration of its market position. Thus, a company should establish its position in the target market by producing all or most of its products there. Starting production activity in a target market is desirable, particularly if a company has other opportunities to enter neighboring countries with its partner.

Figure 7-1. A Simple Checklist for Products

- Is there a need or demand?
- Can the product be produced in the target market?
- Can we distribute efficiently?
- Can we price the product attractively?
- Can our partner play the needed critical roles?
- Can we compete with local competition (if any)?
- Can we preempt future competition for a while?

A company must reexamine its production procedures if it are going to produce its products in a target market. A company must answer a series of key questions affirmatively:

- Do we have the raw materials needed for the finished product?
- Do we have the proper technology for production?
- Do we have the product modified for local needs?
- Do we have the energy for technical production?

Of these four key questions, the third is particularly important. The importance of offering products that are suitable for the market cannot be overstated. Although more will be stated at the end of the chapter, here are three subquestions: First, is the product cost-efficient? In other words, is the product inexpensive to produce, in addition to inexpensive operate? Second, is the product fuel-efficient? For some products (such as tractors, small vehicles, and household appliances), fuel and energy efficiency is critical. Third, is the product functionally efficient? In other words, is the product easy to operate and maintain? Some products, such as computers, can be complicated to operate and maintain for certain less developed markets. All of these questions are critical considerations.

The third item in Figure 7-1 is related to distribution of the product. This topic will be discussed in more detail in Chapters 8 and 9. Suffice it to say that unless a company makes plans about how to distribute its product, the company will have difficulty proceeding.

Whether a company can price its product attractively enough so the target market can afford it is the next critical concern. If the company's products are going to be produced in the target market, could a partner play the necessary role in the company's activities, including production at reasonable costs?

Is there local competition now? If so, can a company compete successfully? A company needs to ask these two questions and answer them affirmatively in order to succeed.

In analyzing competition, future competition must be evaluated also. Will there be other companies with similar ideas? Will there be enough room for everyone? What if a local company starts competing by pirating products? In other words, a company should be reasonably sure that competition will be preempted for a short while. One way of preempting competition is by establishing a strong market position. Of course, this fact is almost a given since a company enters a market from the low end and relies on large quantities sold in that particular market.

DISTINGUISHING A PRODUCT

To establish a strong market position, a company must accept that its product is distinguished and recognized. In addition to product characteristics, two additional features play an important role in distribution of a product: country of origin and brand name. Two examples stand out as historic developments. Bayer aspirin and Singer sewing machines have been around for a long time. These two products entered the remotest corners of the world. They became established as reputable products and continue to be successful. Bayer aspirin, a unique product developed in Germany, has penetrated all markets of the world. Singer also came up with a much-needed product. Since clothing is produced at home in most parts of the world, a sewing machine improves individual productivity. Hand-manipulated and foot-pedal sewing machines are of great value in remote corners of the world where there is no electricity.

COUNTRY OF ORIGIN VERSUS BRAND

As you read in the above examples, the country of origin is very important in generating a reputation for a company. In certain less developed countries, just owning a product generated in the West conveys status. Any U.S. product in Mexico is considered superior. However, in third-world countries, certain middle-class consumers believe in using domestic products. In such cases, the emphasis is not on the country of origin, but the brand. A product may be given a domestic name, and the product may be the beginning of a series of products with local brand names. In fact, if a third-world middle class happens to be a target market and if no other attempt is made to reach that market, a company may find that its partner's brand is more appropriate to promote. If neither a company's name nor its partner's name is well known at start-up, the company must depend on the distributors' or storekeepers' efforts to promote the product. Storekeepers who carry a product, particularly when it is first introduced play an important role in promoting a product.

At start-up, a company must decide whether it wants to emphasize the country of origin, where the product originated, its brand, or its partner's brand. Once a decision is made, the company must stick with it. The company's decision impacts consumer learning.

CONSUMER LEARNING, CONSUMER INVOLVEMENT, AND CONSUMER LOYALTY

Low levels of literacy, limited mass media exposure, and traditions of high-context cultures make consumer learning difficult in third-world markets. But the fact still remains that consumers must learn about products, brand, and so on. If consumers don't know a company's products and our brand, how can they make repeat purchases? A company must find a way to enhance consumer learning.

As you know, consumers in third-world countries live and function in high-context cultures. These consumers also typically belong to collectivistic societies. In both types of cultural classifications, consumer interaction and group influences are critical. Consumers in such cultures are influenced by others—family elders, opinion leaders, and storekeepers.

Storekeepers are particularly important when consumers are directly involved in a product's characteristics or features. In most less developed countries, consumers have a limited income; therefore, they want to make wise buying choices. In such cases, particularly when deciding whether to purchase more expensive and more sophisticated products, consumers may try out a product. With the storekeeper's help, consumers can be more involved and acquire more information from the storekeeper directly.

In third-world countries, consumers often buy a product for the extended family. Family elders and storekeepers—in other words, people rather than mass media or written communication—influence the purchase decisions (Samli 1995). Buying among human interaction and buying for a group may not create product or brand loyalty for the individual consumer. However, buyers may develop inertia, in which case they buy the same products automatically without question. This type of blind loyalty to a product or brand can last a long time; blind loyalty can also come to a sudden halt. Thus, loyalty becomes an important factor.

LOYALTY TO WHOM?

Although brand name is used to identify a product, consumer loyalty is likely to be to a storekeeper and elders, who are not likely to change their minds unless they are totally dissatisfied with a product. Thus, satisfaction provided by a product feeds into and enhances the inertia that may have emerged. Part of a consumer's satisfaction stems from the service provided by a company.

HOW MUCH SERVICE, WHAT KIND, BY WHOM?

The more technical the product, the greater the need for service. After all, the market segment may not be very sophisticated. Customers may need information about how to use the product. They may also need information to maintain the product. They may need even more information and service to repair the product. Whether the company provides the service or a partner performs this job does not change the fact that service must be offered.

WHERE THE LOCAL PARTNER SHINES

If a local partner can perform the service requirement of the target market and the partner performs well, the result can be synergistic in terms of establishing market power. The local partner can shine like a hero, particularly if service is good and affordable. Since labor is not very costly, a win-win situation results. However, the more complicated the product, the greater the need for training the service providers.

THE COMPANY DOES THE TRAINING:

When Union Carbide built a factory in India, training was done by the locals. The result was the Bhopal incident. An explosion (due to inadequate training) caused massive damage, and thousands of people died or were injured. The whole episode cost Union Carbide billions of dollars. Not every endeavor into foreign markets is that complicated or risky, but training must be provided and must be done well. Two key goals are pursued: consistency and quality.

SERVICE CONSISTENCY AND UNIFORM QUALITY

In third-world countries, service, in general, is not a concern; it is inconsistent and of questionable quality. Therefore, a company can train its partner's service providers to give consistently high-quality and uniform service, the company's market power will be so much stronger. In other words, service can be one of the strengths that differentiates a company in the marketplace.

In addition to the service element, which is closely related to the nature of the physical product, the physical features of the product are critical in a third-world market.

THE PHYSICAL PRODUCT

Figure 7-2 explores some of the more important aspects of a company's products and their suitability to target market conditions. Size is the most important physical feature that needs to be considered. Since space is limited in consumers' home as well as in stores, a product's size is an important consideration. Appliances in Eastern Europe are small because people live in very small quarters. Stores in most less developed countries are small with limited storage space. Storekeepers are cognizant of space limitations directly related to product size.

A company must determine the extent to which it can produce its products without importing parts and components from other places, particularly when the product line is technical. Raw materials are closely connected to the components issue. However, in some cases, the finished product requires local raw materials. If, for instance, a company has a small

Figure 7-2. Functional Arrangements

Features	Impact
Size	Suitability of the product to available space
Components	Being able to use domestic resources
Raw materials	Being able to use the product with domestic raw materials
Cost efficiency	Being able to produce the product efficiently an can run the product efficiently
Consistency with other products	Ability of the product to interact
Quality	Measured primarily by longevity

home apparatus to generate peanut butter but the country does not grow peanuts or a small machine for producing woolen products at home but the country does not produce wool, the feasibility of the company's product becomes questionable. Cost efficiency is related to productivity of the production process and more importantly, to how much energy, water, and other resources the product requires when being used. Without cost efficiency, a product does not have much of a chance of surviving in the target markets. The product simply is not generating consumer value.

If a company's product is not consistent with other products, the company has a serious problem. For instance, if the market uses the metric system but a company's product does not, the company is not likely to succeed. A product must be consistent with other products in a given setting.

Finally, quality, which in limited-income markets is measured by the durability or longevity of a product, must be such that consumers notice it and communicate it to others. More than anything else, the combination of cost efficiency with durability determines a company's level of success. They mean value in emerging markets.

SUMMARY

This chapter deals with what a company offers in the market. If goods and services do not promise value to consumers, a company does not have a chance to survive. A checklist can be used to see if the market is a good match for a company. If a company cannot produce, distribute, or price its product attractively or if there is no demand for the produce, the company is not likely to succeed. A company expects its partner to play a major role. This role becomes particularly important if a company is using the partner's name and if the partner is providing valuable production and service functions.

In third-world countries, consumer learning is closely related to direct involvement. However, consumers are also influenced by opinion leaders and/or storekeepers as they buy for the group or extended family. Once consumers are used to a product, inertia sets in; they buy almost automatically.

Finally, the physical features of a product or product line are critical. If a product is cost-efficient and lasts a long time, a company will have a strong market position.

REFERENCES

Samli, A. Coskun (1995). International Consumer Behavior. Westport, CT: Quorum Books.

8

Reaching the Consumer Physically

D istribution channels in the industrialized world are well-organized, fully functioning institutional pathways through which products move from the manufacturer or producer to the consumer or user.

In third-world countries, distribution channels are not the same as they are in the industrialized world. Some functions of distribution channels are duplicated, and some functions, which are expected, are not performed. Furthermore, the functions of the channel performed by its members are garbled up; wholesalers may be retailers, retailers may be wholesalers and so on. Also, other institutions in the channel are not available in the channels of industrialized countries. One such institution is street vendors. In third-world markets, there are many street vendors that are controlled and dispatched by a commissioner or another agent. In third-world countries, bringing retailing closer to the consumer may take a type of street-vending activity since there may not be many retail outlets, particularly near poor parts of town.

The dispatcher, agent, or commissioner is in touch with street vendors, who can then bring the product closer to the consumer. In rural sections of third-world countries, this aspect of the channel may be critical for the distribution of a product.

The other alternative is the bazaar. Traditionally there are two types of bazaars, permanent and rotating. Permanent bazaars are somewhat similar to the U.S. version of the flea market, except permanent bazaars have a combination of vendor stalls and retail stores. Rotating bazaars are vendors who come to a flea market periodically, once a week or so. Visiting the rotating bazaars is a family outing, similar to a combination picnic and county fair.

A company knowing that distribution channels are not the same everywhere and that in third-world countries, they are not as clear as the channels in industrial markets is not enough. A company must also be aware of the unique features of many of the distribution systems that exist in a target market. Then a decision must be made with regard to the contextual nature of the distribution activity a company is planning so it can choose the most appropriate distribution system for its product. If a company is not clear as to how it will distribute its product, the company will have difficultly choosing the most appropriate distribution channel.

HIGH-CONTEXT DISTRIBUTION

High-context and low-context cultures were discussed earlier. Almost all developed countries have high-context cultures, meaning that people's interaction is important in the sale of a product. If street peddlers or retail storekeepers do not encourage he purchase of a product, family elders and opinion leaders do. In all of these cases, communication between the buyer and the seller is critical. Interpersonal influences are the crux of high-context distribution. Where and how will consumers be exposed to communications that lead them in the direction of a purchase? The need for the distribution channel to provide interaction and communication with the customer is great, particularly when a product (say, a home appliance or home improvement supplies) requires some explanation as to how it should be used and how it should be maintained. This concept is known as high-context distribution.

WHY NOT LOW-CONTEXT DISTRIBUTION?

Third-world countries have high-context cultures. In such situations, a low-context distribution system, self-service, telemarketing, e-trade catalogue sales, and so on, are suitable. Some communication and minor sales pitches take place even when street vendors sell their products. Personal communication, the sales pitch, and certain cultural traditions (such as drinking tea during the negotiation process) are high-context traits. They can be offered only through high-context distribution.

Many well-known products that are sold in developed markets—Calvin Klein, Banana Republic, Benetton, Hilfiger, IBM, and Xerox—have direct marketing channels. Products reach the consumer or the user through a company-owned distribution system or through the distribution system they directly negotiate with and with whom they come to a joint agreement. This is called direct distribution.

DIRECT VERSUS INDIRECT

In direct distribution, a company plans its distribution activity specifically and distributes its products through its own distribution system, its own retailers, and its own distribution centers and wholesalers. In indirect distribution, a company does not own the components of the distribution channel and often does not make detailed plans for its distribution activity. Somebody else does these tasks, such as export management companies or export trading companies (Samli and Hill 1998).

A small- or medium-size firm is not likely to enter a third-world market with a direct distribution system. The company cannot afford a distribution system that it owns totally. The company cannot create a chain of retail establishments or a series of distribution centers. Thus, it enters a market by indirect distribution. In other words, someone else makes the distribution decisions and manages the distribution activity. The most logical candidate for this activity is the partner.

A company must address at least six key questions to assess its partner's capabilities regarding a distribution system or to assess another third party's capabilities hired by the partner. Figure 8-1 presents these questions and their implications.

First, a company needs to explore whether the partner can reach and cultivate the target market adequately. After all, if a product does not reach prospective customers, the company cannot be successful in the market. One way to answer this question is to determine a partner's past experience in distributing products in the market. If a partner has the necessary experience, both parties win. However, success still depends on whether the partner's past experience and its existing distribution system can be used for a company's product. If not, the company should look for a new partner.

Even if the existing distribution system of a partner seems suitable for a company's products, there is still room for improvement. In a high-context culture, a company must ask whether

Figure 8-1. Performance of the Distribution System

Key Issue	Implication
• Does our partner have a good outreach?	Our market is cultivated adequately.
• Is our partner's distribution system working well?	Our partner has the necessary experience.
• Can the same distribution system be used for our products?	This may not be the right partner.
• Is there enough opportunity for high-context distribution?	There is human interaction throughout.
• Do consumers have recourse to ask questions or replace the product?	Market power is established through reliability.
• Do we have early indicators showing the the performance of the distribution system?	We are able to revise and improve.

enough opportunity exists for high-context distribution. The company needs to know if there is enough human interaction in its distribution activity. Are customers able to talk to people in the distribution system about the product and its care? Based on human interaction needs, high-context cultures require high-context distribution systems. These systems allows customers to interact with storekeepers and with others at all times.

The question customers have recourse when they question the merits of a product or want to replace it. This service establishes market power for a company since it is not available in third-world countries.

Finally, do early indicators show that the performance of a distribution system is more than adequate? If performance is less than adequate, this fact needs to be known quickly so accompany can revise and improve its distribution system.

Even though a company distributes its product indirectly (i.e., a partner is in charge), the firm has reasonable control over distribution through the partner's activities. However, particularly in third-world markets, other buyers from other groups (through their own initiative) may buy and distribute the company's products, say, among their own few retail establishments. For instance, if a company distributes its home improvement products with Group A that has five stores, in an adjacent area of town, Group B unexpectedly approaches the company to buy products to sell in its three stores. With Group A, the company made arrangements for service and delivery and other procedures; with Group B, the company made no such agreements. Thus, problems may arise as signals get crossed.

WHAT IF THE SIGNALS GET CROSSED?

In the above case, if A's transactions and procedures are very different from what B is doing, the company's position in the market may become shaky. If, for instance, Group B does not follow the philosophy of giving consumers recourse to ask questions, to replace products, or to complain and if Group B charges a lot more or a lot less than Group A, the company sends mixed messages to the market, and the signals get crossed.

Although the partner may be anxious to sell to Group B, unless the same signals are sent to the market, a company may do more harm than good to sales and to the company name. In third-world markets, where money is scarce and human interaction is more readily present, not having consistency in product offering can be harmful to a company.

In developed countries, it may be damaging to have the same product in two or more different retail stores. For example, the name Calvin Klein and its value is likely to diminish if the same Calvin Klein products are found in a chain of expensive boutiques as well as in a chain of discount or convenience stores. In the markets of developing countries, since consumers are more scattered and distribution channels may not be working well, how consumes finding a product is moot as long as the discrepancy (if any) in the offering is not noticeable.

One additional factor a company needs to keep in mind is the third-party distributor. A partner may have an independent distributor. Although the two may work together successfully, the third-party distributor will not concern itself with following a company's conditions unless the firm makes sure its philosophy is honored. What if a partner is functioning in an adjacent foreign market? It may be a good opportunity for a company to enter that market; however, the third-party distributor becomes even more of an issue since the partner, no doubt, is using nationals in the adjacent market for distribution. This third-party distributor may not believe it has any obligation to follow the company's instructions or philosophy. Thus, conditions may become difficult for the company to establish its distribution conditions and to implement them.

ALTERNATIVE DISTRIBUTION SYSTEMS

Now that you have looked at the variations in the distribution systems in third-world countries, we can put the whole picture together. Figure 8-2 presents the alternative distribution systems that we can choose from. The critical part of the Figure is the retailing end. Department stores exist in major metropolitan areas in third-world countries. The stores are somewhat similar to their U.S. counterparts. Department stores in third-world countries are developing their own branches at the outskirts of the metropolitan areas. These branches are much smaller and carry much less variety.

Retail stores are typically small stores near or part of apartment complexes or living quarters. The stores are specialized and carry little variety. One store specializes in fresh vegetables, another in breads and cakes, another in meats, another in apparel, and so on.

Permanent bazaars are located in the center of smaller towns. They are smaller version of American flea markets. A

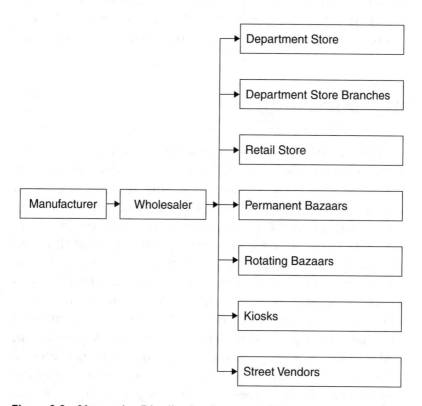

Figure 8-2. Alternative Distribution Systems in Third-World Countries

rotating bazaar is a temporary flea market that sets up on specific days of the week. It is typically located adjacent to but outside of small towns and sometimes between towns.

Kiosks are common in places that have a lot of pedestrian traffic. Kiosks provide continuity to the consumer by carrying certain products. Consumers know they can buy a certain product from a particular kiosk when they need to.

Street vendors are a way to bring products to the consumer. Since consumers in third-world countries do not usually have their own means of transportation and public transportation is not adequate, bringing products to the consumer can be effective for a company.

A company must understand the alternative distribution systems that exist in third-world countries so it can decide which system will provide the best product distribution. Although a partner may have vast experience, the company must look at the situation from its perspective. The company must look at the pluses and minuses on the basis of its goals and aspirations.

SUMMARY

Distribution channels are not the same everywhere, and a company must understand the differences. In third-world markets, where high-context cultures prevail, the distribution system must accommodate the culture's needs. Consumers need to interact with people at select points so they can receive information, raise questions, and return the merchandise (if necessary). Whether a company distributes directly or indirectly is another key issue it must resolve. The chances are that the partner will make that decision, but a company needs to understand the partner's point of view in this regard. It is expected that a company will use indirect distribution. A problem in third-world countries is that different distributors may attempt to distribute a company's products, and their treatment of the products may not be consistent. Whereas one group of distributors may adhere to the conditions inherent in high-context markets, another group may completely ignore the conditions.

A company must understand the alternative distribution systems that exist in third-world countries in order to be successful in the target markets.

REFERENCES

Samli, A. Coskun and Hill, John R. (1998), *Marketing Globally.* Lincolnwood, Illinois: NTC Business Books.

9

Moving the Merchandise
and Passing the Word

Actual handling of a product, whether a company is exporting, producing, or assembling in the target market, is critical. A company must consider the physical movement of finished products from where they are produced to where they are distributed and the movement of raw materials, parts, or components until the product is in its final form.

As was discussed earlier, in third-world countries, high-context cultures prevail. High-context cultures do not pay enough attention to time. "Everything has its own time" is the basic philosophy (Samli 1995). With such a philosophy, it would be difficult to expect an efficient and effective logistics system to perform well in a target market.

Good logistics systems are time-efficient. With good logistics systems in the movements of raw materials, parts, and components, maximum output results from minimum input. But logistics systems also need to be effective, meaning they move the merchandise and cargo to the proper destination and they move the proper merchandise and cargo.

In moving a product from point of manufacturing to point of sale, make sure that the proper amounts of raw materials, parts, or components reach their destination on time. If a logistics system does not function, a company can have serious inventory problems.

INVENTORIES SHOULD NOT BECOME A BOTTLENECK

If a company hopes to have reasonable sales volumes, it needs inventories to support the sales volumes. In other words, if a company does not have supplies, it cannot sell. Having adequate supplies implies that a company has adequate storage too, as meaning the company can handle the merchandise adequately as it moves closer to the consumer.

A company should not assume that its partner has a good logistics system and that the partner is concerned with efficiency. If the retailers (or whoever will be carrying the products and selling them to consumers) do not have adequate inventories, they cannot sell. The opposite is also a problem. If the retailers get more than adequate inventories, this becomes a costly proposition. Thus, over or under-stocked holdings of retailers become a serious bottleneck. The critical issue is to make sure that reasonable stocks are created and maintained at all points of our distribution system. These inventories must reflect a reasonable just-in-time system.

JUST IN TIME FOR WHAT?

"Just in time" is a commonly used concept in logistics. If a product has many parts and one or two of those parts is missing during assembly, the whole process is delayed. The process is efficient only when the parts are available when needed. In our target market ports, the concept of "just in time" may not be understood or considered important. If products do not reach the market on time, they cannot be sold on time. Even if a partner is time-conscious, means of transportation (i.e., roads, vehicles, waterways, and railroads) may not be in shape for optimal use; hence, just-in-time objectives may not materialize because of deficient transportation.

QUICK RESPONSE IS CRITICAL

Products need to be available and ready just in time, but it is also important that a company respond to market needs quickly. Quick response is critical if the market is sending a negative message about a product, if the market cannot get enough of a product, or if the product is damaged or is spoiled when it is delivered. Since retailers do not have adequate facilities for storage, companies must commit to just-in-time and quick response. If a business is successful, a distribution center that has adequate inventory and outreach possibilities can be developed in the near future. An illustration of the importance of logistics is not having a blood bank in central African countries. Not only is refrigeration in short supply; poor roads and undependable transportation are a fact of life.

If a company is planning to expand into a large area, the company must consider third-party logistics and, above all, outsourcing.

OUTSOURCING FOR PROFIT AND MARKET POWER

Assume, for instance, that a company sells an efficient washer-dryer. A partner assembles and produces some of the parts; the company outsources production of the parts the partner does not produce. Outsourcing is important to a company because it depends on the outsourcing activity. Therefore, the company must carefully examine the qualifications of the prospective source. Figure 9-1 sets forth the criteria that can be used to evaluate outsourcing prospects.

Figure 9-1. Criteria for Evaluating Outsourcing

- How long has the prospective source been in business?
- What kind of reputation does the prospective source have?
- Has the prospective source done business with the company's partner?
- Can the company see samples of the prospective source's output?
- Can the company sign an airtight outsourcing agreement?
- Does the prospective source need additional information?
- Can the prospective source deliver varying levels of output?
- Can the company count on quality?
- Can the company count on price?
- Will the name of the prospective source enhance acceptance of the company's finished product?

How long a prospective source has been in business is important because a company must look at the track record of that source. Without a track record, a company cannot evaluate a prospective source.

How long the source has been functioning and what kind of reputation it has are related. If a company is going to do business with a source, the company needs to make sure that the source has a good reputation.

If a company's partner has already done business with a prospective source, the company can be reassured. A company can be encouraged by a partner's positive experience with a third party.

Despite a good reputation and a partner's positive experiences, a company may wish to see samples of the prospective source's output. The company's engineers can evaluate whether the output is suitable to its product characteristics.

Signing a contract with a prospective source that is mutually satisfactory is an important risk-reducing factor. If such a contract can be developed and agreed upon, some risk is eliminated. However, in third-world countries, a handshake is more important than a contract.

A company cannot assume that a prospective source has a sufficient technological background. Hence, the question comes up as to the technological needs of the third party. Does a company have the proper technology, and can the transfer that technology successfully?

Since economic conditions are somewhat volatile, a company must find out if a prospective source can deliver varying levels of outputs. The economy may be booming, and the company may be selling a lot more of its product than originally planned. If a source cannot deliver the extra parts or components needed, the company will miss out on an important opportunity.

When needed quantities vary, quality may also vary. However, a company cannot tolerate inconsistencies in quality. A source must be able to provide consistence.

In addition to quality, a company also must consider price. If a prospective source increases its prices when demand goes up, a company may have difficulty establishing itself as a reliable company. The company will have to raise prices to absorb the losses.

Finally, but equally important, does the name of a source enhance the image a company is projecting? Consumer acceptance of a finished product can be enhanced if a company's source has a good name of its own. A company should take advantage of such a synergistic opportunity.

Thus, careful analysis of a prospective source can improve a company's opportunity for profit and market power. Outsourcing can be a powerful move. It can benefit all parties involved as it contributes to the creation of consumer value.

When a company is dealing with the markets where the forgotten majority lives, third-party logistics is an important concept.

THIRD-PARTY LOGISTICS

A partner may have multiple talents but may not have its own logistics capabilities. Still, raw materials, parts, components, and finished products need to be moved and made available to the consumer. In such cases, a company needs a logistics specialist who can handle all aspects of moving merchandise to the consumer. Since time and efficiency are not priorities in third-world countries, logistics are not advanced. A company may have difficulty finding a specialist to handle third-party logistics. A company may need to help create such an organization by bringing more than one transportation company together.

As a company's product moves through the channels and gets closer to prospective customers, the company needs to communicate with the market. After all, if a product is in the stores but consumers don't know about it, the product will not sell.

COMMUNICATING WITH THE MASSES

Since mass media is not well developed and since literacy is low in third-world markets, communication with the market must begin early. Although newspapers are the most common medium, they may not be the best choice for a company wanting to get its message out. Illiteracy limits newspaper advertising. In third-world countries, because of high-context cultural characteristics, human interaction is important. Therefore, communicating with the market is primarily dependent upon personal contact and audiovisual communication such as TV and radio. TV ownership tends to be low; as a result, radio is the best medium for mass communication. However, storekeepers' interactions with people is the key to influencing consumers. This is an important consideration for doing promotions. High-context cultures are skeptical about new things. Therefore, storekeepers' assurances play an important role in eliminating consumer skepticism.

Communicating with the market is critical; however, the content of the communication is what really count. A company must decide what the keys to its communication are and how the message be composed and carried out.

THE KEY TO COMMUNICATION

When attempting to communicate with the market, a company must consider four key areas: product versus brand image; the building of a reputation for a halo effect, personal contacts; and brochures, packages, and storekeepers.

PRODUCT VERSUS BRAND IMAGE

A company must decide early on whether it will emphasize the product connected to the company name or develop a brand. If a company has plans to expand its product line in such a way that a series of unrelated products are introduced into the market, the company should refrain from using the company's name. Introducing unrelated products is similar to sending out contradictory messages. As a result, a company may create a credibility gap for itself. Similar groups of products should be connected to different family brands with which local consumers are comfortable. Then these family brands are marketed separately.

Brand versus Reputation
The brand name that a company develops and the reputation of the company or its partner are two critical aspects of communication that can work together to create synergy or that can work against each other.

Figure 9-2 illustrates the relationship between these two concepts. Although a brand is not yet well established, a company should be aiming at the upper left quadrant. A company's communication efforts must go in this direction.

THE BUILDING OF REPUTATION FOR A HALO EFFECT

Developing a positive reputation is critical since emotionalism is prevalent in third-world countries. Such emotionalism creates a very strong attachment to a product or brand. If a brand

Brand

	Strong	Weak
Strong **Company Reputation**	Strong market position exists because of synergism.	Brand is not well known yet. But with company name, the brand is strong enough.
 Weak	Company reputation is interfering with the brand.	This is the worst of the situations. Do not proceed.

Figure 9-2. Brand versus Reputation

name becomes a household word, introducing other products under the same brand is feasible and profitable for a company. This is what is meant by the "halo effect." The stronger a brand, the stronger the halo effect that improves the probability of success for new products. However, a company must look at the issues if it introduces a number of unrelated products. The products may be grouped into different brand names, which has positive and negative aspects.

PERSONAL CONTACT AS PROMOTION

In addition to the role emotionalism plays and the emphasis on human interaction, third-world markets present an opportunity to promote products or our name as part of personal communications. Figure 9-3 illustrates the role of personal contact. Being collectivistic, not individualistic, third-world cultures thrive on interaction among people. But more importantly, different opinion leaders influence these interaction processes in different settings. Collectivistic cultures influence individuals as members of a group; therefore, a group's influence on an individual is profound. Each group has its own opinion leaders. In family affairs, this influence extends into consumption pat-

Figure 9-3. Personal Contact as Promotion

terns. Family elders, the family doctor, certain wise people in networks in which individuals participate, and storekeepers as a source of information about products and consumption habits are all opinion leaders. A company's responsibility, depending on its product line, is to identify and communicate with opinion leaders, who, in turn, communicate with consumers.

Communication with consumers is a major part of a company's promotional activity in a high-context environment. Depending on its distribution system and planned sales volume, a company may decide to have conversations with storekeepers to improve their knowledge about products. A company must be factual and informative about its products if it wants to make an impact in this high-context culture. But what about other types of communication? Because of high illiteracy, newspapers are a poor choice. However, since in many third-world countries, radio is national rather than local, national radio can be used. What about brochures, packages, and the like?

BROCHURES, PACKAGES, AND OTHER MEANS OF COMMUNICATION

Because of high literacy, a company may decide not to use brochures unless they are illustrated with pictures and use simple writing. However, packages or containers can be the first line of communication with the consumers. And by using illustrations, pictures, and logos, a company can enhance its communication with the market through packages or containers.

In third-world countries, where money is scarce, human interaction is important, and the level of literacy is low, the influence of others has the biggest impact. But this does not preclude the use of local mass media by a company. Although newspapers are low in cost and accessible to consumers, because of the high level of illiteracy, newspaper advertising may not be suitable. Furthermore, newspapers in many third-world countries are numerous and represent certain political affiliations. Therefore, while they may be appropriate for market segmentation, they cannot be effectively used for reaching out to the general second or third tier of the market.

Certain local mass media that must be used. Among these are posters displaying products and the company's name and signs in public transportation vehicles and stations. Unlike newspapers, radio can be good for making general announcements and blanketing the market with messages. Television and the Internet are not useful; not enough people own TVs and computers. But stationary kiosks and street vendors can be used to reinforce a company's image and brand. Finally, movie theatres are useful for the same purpose. Since television ownership is not common, consumers like to go to movies; hence, movie theaters hold captive audiences with which a company can communicate. A company can present a short movie clip set in local surroundings using local personalities, which may be more influential than many other media.

An emphasis on audiovisual as opposed to written communication is natural. However, audiovisual communication does not go as far as human interaction in third-world countries. As a result, opinion leaders play a critical role in a company's attempts to communicate with the market.

Thus far, the Internet is not widely used in third-world countries. The small minorities that are engaged in Internet purchasing are not part of a company's target market. It will take many years before the Internet becomes an important communication medium.

As for the use of multimedia, a company must ensure that the messages carried by different media are consistent. When a company is trying to establish a strong brand or corporate image and the messages are not consistent, the market will not take the company seriously, resulting in an early credibility gap. However, this does not mean that, once started, the message cannot be changed. Feedback may indicate that a message is not effective. In such cases, a company needs to develop a new message. But development needs to be slow and gradual since emotional implications of communications are far-reaching in these cultures.

THE BEGINNING OF THE COMMUNICATION PROCESS

When there is limited availability of manufactured goods, the presence of a seller's market, and minimal competition, the introduction of a company's product and its name needs to be tailored to the prevailing socioeconomic environment. Making an impact early on can create the needed wave of communication. But a company may need to supply the infrastructure necessary to promote its products to the market. Here are some examples:

- In Kenya, Coca Cola supplies refrigerators to dealers in rural areas so consumers can buy cold drinks.
- In Nigeria, some international firms subsidize the purchase of generators by their local distributors.
- In Nigeria, Johnson & Johnson used vans with loudspeakers.
- In Columbia, Warner and Lambert used over 30,000 street vendors to sell its chewing gum products.
- In Papua, New Guinea, a live theater was used to introduce a number of products.
- Demonstration teams visited town squares to demonstrate products. After the demonstrations (and free samples), point-of-purchase displays were set up in critical places.

These and many other promotional activities can create high recall and retention of promotional messages. With the lack of competition, such dramatic introductions can create strong brand loyalty (Fletcher and Melewar 2001, Arnold and Quelch 1998).

SUMMARY

This chapter explores two critical functions of a business, logistics and communication.

Moving merchandise from the raw material stage to the point where it is ready to be used or consumed is critical. The actual handling of merchandise is not only an important cost factor, but also an important time factor. Products must be at the point of sale on time. Since third-world markets do not pay much attention to time, logistics plays a critical role.

When a company is dealing with logistics, outsourcing is an issue that may emerge. With complex finished products that have many parts and components, there is the question of using local suppliers. A checklist may be used that enables a company to evaluate a prospective source. A company cannot expect a partner to single-handedly take care of the logistics of the business. In fact, an outside third-party logistics company may be necessary. However, because logistics is not advanced in third-world countries, a company may need to create a logistics company to do the job.

A company's communication with the market and promotion of its products and itself are done differently in third-world markets. Being primarily high-context cultures, the emphasis is on human interaction and personal communication. A company may decide to promote brands if it has multiple products and plans to introduce new ones. Opinion leaders are the most important means of communication. In the case of using multiple communication media, within the constraints of third-world markets, a company's message must be consistent.

One of the most important considerations of a company attempting to communicate with the market is trying to make a good first impression. With the absence of infrastructure and a lack of competition, a company must think differently when dealing with a third-world market than when attempting to enter more industrialized market.

REFERENCES

Arnold, David J. and Quelch, John A. (1998). "New Strategies in Emerging Markets," *Sloan Management Review*, Fall, 7-20.

Fletcher, Richard and Melewar, T.C. (2001). "The complexities of communicating to customers in Emerging Markets," *Journal of Communication Management*, Sept., 9-22.

Samli, A. Coskun (1995). *International Consumer Behavior*, Westport, Connecticut: Quorum Books.

10

The Value of
Products and Services

I f a product or service is going to be successful in a market,
it must generate value for the consumer. This particular
point pertains even more so to third-world markets, since
consumers have limited means. They do not have much, if any,
discretionary income, so a product must make a positive difference in consumers' lives. Thus, the value of a product is
extremely important. In the West, price usually indicates value;
this is not the case in third-world markets.

Price-perceived quality is a Western cultural value. The concept of quality takes on a different meaning in third-world markets. Quality in these markets equates to durability and
functional performance. Since money is scarce, people do not
like to make repeat purchases even though new and more
attractive models are available. Thus, it is not price-perceived
quality that is important, but price and quality.

If a product lasts a long time, is reasonably priced, performs
well, and is economical to operate, a company has an opportunity to make a positive impact on the local market. Therefore, a
company is not exploiting of the market by charging as much as
the market will bear. Trying to sell as much as possible is what
works in third-world markets. Stated differently, a company

should not enter the market using high-end niche marketing based only on the well-off few. Rather, a company should enter using low-end mass marketing to second, third, and fourth tiers.

PRICING FOR PENETRATION

If a company does not use price-perceived quality and skim pricing due to very limited markets composed of relatively well-off consumers, the natural alternative is penetration pricing. A company must price its product in such a way that it will penetrate the market. The bigger a company's attempts to penetrate the market, the greater the probability of making more money. Simultaneously, if a product has penetrated the market and the product or brand name has become well known, loyalty to the product increases. This situation improves a company's chances to preempt future competition. A strong market position will discourage future competitors from entering the market. As you can see, penetration pricing not only improves a company's chances to make more money, it also improves the company's market position against prospective competition.

Two additional features of penetration pricing strategy are important as well. First, if a partner or a third party is producing (fully or partially) a company's products, large volumes of production, up to a point, means economies of scale. In other words, up to a certain point, when a company produces more, overall costs go down for each additional unit produced. Hence, penetration pricing generates more profits.

Second, again if a product is partially or fully produced in the target market and if a company uses penetration pricing, the firm will employ more local labor. The French economist Jean Baptiste Say articulated a concept known as Say's Law. Say's Law states that supply creates its own demand. This is particularly applicable to third-world countries. A company's efforts to produce more creates a modest but important growth in the economy. This impact has a ripple effect and creates further expansion in the income base, which directly or indirectly benefits the business. The ripple effect expands the economic base. There is more employment and more income, and part of this expanding economic base used by locals to buy the company's product.

Since interaction among people is common in high-context cultures, consumers in these countries must be given an opportunity to negotiate price. Money also being rather scarce, they have an additional incentive to negotiate.

FLEXIBLE PRICING

If human interaction is important and people have more time than money, negotiation is natural. Of course, for negotiation to take place, prices must be somewhat flexible. In the industrialized West, prices are fixed, allowing no room for negotiations. But the opposite is true for third-world markets. In some countries, negotiation is a common past time. Businesspeople in retail stores enjoy negotiating and becoming friends with customers so they will see repeat sales. Further into the countryside, even less money is in the hands of consumers. They need to negotiate even more vigorously. Thus, the further a company penetrates into a market, the more flexible its prices need to be.

It is reasonable to believe that there is a substantial reservoir of pent-up demand in remote parts of rural markets (Arnold and Quelch 1998). This pent-up demand will surface as products are made available and prices become affordable.

With regard to price, product service must be considered. In the West, service for a product's repair, maintenance, and parts is important. However, in third-world markets, the actual price of a product may be more important. Service is an additional factor a company can use to enter a market to establish recognizable market power. All in all, a company's approach to pricing our product must generate substantial consumer value. This means that instead of trying to maximize profits through skim pricing, a company should generate consumer value by using penetration pricing. In the long run, this approach yields high profits. Remember penetration pricing is based on a low unit price and high volume. Thus, cost savings due to larger volumes must be passed on to the consumer to facilitate greater penetration into the market.

TARGET MARKET CURRENCY CONSIDERATIONS

The target market is likely to have a soft currency, meaning that the legal tender has no value outside of the country.

A company will want to take its profits (partially or fully) out of the country. Typically, a company has made arrangements with its bank at home and the central bank of the country. But the government of the target market must agree to the arrangement so the company can take its earnings out of the country.

When dealing with soft currencies, a company must be cognizant of at least two facts. First, the target market probably has a greater rate of inflation than the United States. This implies that, unchecked, prices could skyrocket. Second, as U.S. dollars become more expensive because of domestic inflation in the target country, the price of a product may go up even though the product is entirely domestically produced with no imported components, parts, or materials. In this case, a company must try to minimize the price increase due to artificial inflation (artificial in that it is indirect and not related to supply and demand). If a company allows prices to go very high, the market will lose confidence. Thus, to a certain extent, keeping the price line low enhances market power and customer loyalty.

If a target country's currency is soft and good payment agreements are not achieved, countertrading may become an alternative. Some firms have established certain barter or countertrading arrangements. For example, a woman in the United States began importing used kimonos from Japan. In return, she sent used blue jeans to Japan. The kimonos were reconditioned. Those that could not be used were made into lampshades and pillowcases. The blue jeans were altered to fit Japanese consumers. Subsequently, she owned multiple stores in the United States and Japan.

Countertrading can be a profitable venture. Arranging for countertrading requires responding to a series of questions, presented in Figure 10-1. Answers to these questions tell a company if it is worthwhile to consider such an activity.

BARTERING POSSIBILITIES

The first question in Figure 10-1 goes to the heart of the issue. Many years ago Coca Cola bartered its products with Hungarian wines and Bulgarian calculators. Many similar arrangements have taken place over the years. If the target-market country has certain products that the home market would find be valuable, barter possibilities exist. When a company can use the soft money made in the target market in exchange for these products, the barter system is likely to work smoothly.

Figure 10-1. Bartering Possibilities

Key Questions	Positive Outcomes
Does the target market have certain products that are valuable at home?	Not only does the company settle its problem with soft currency, it makes more money.
Can the soft money made from these products be easily exchanged?	The result is a smoothly functioning barter arrangement.
Can these products be marketed at home?	The company generates additional revenue.
Should a third party be involved at home to buy or market these products?	Profit is reduced, but so are major headaches.
Might this kind of bartering come under fire?	This arrangement is not a short-run solution.
Could professional bartering companies help?	At least for the interim period, things run smoothly.

Having acquired the products that may be desirable at home is not enough. Can a company market them at home? This situation can generate additional revenue if effective marketing at home is developed. If a company cannot market the product, it may look to find a third party to carry the marketing responsibilities and generate an effective marketing process. Any revenues the company shares with the third party may be offset by additional revenues brought in by the third party. This proposition eliminates any problems for a company trying to market the bartered products itself at home.

Just what are the potential barriers to a bartering proposition? Although there may not be any major barriers presently, problems can come up in the future. But if a company is able to anticipate problems, might the company consult with another firm experienced in advising? An interesting proposition here is the possibility of a company having a few bartering arrangements simultaneously when it is functioning in more than one market. This is called switch trading, and it means that multiple parties are involved in countertrading simultaneously with one another. Switch trading can be rather lucrative. However, it can divert a company's attention from its core activities. Although switch trading is a challenge, it can also be an opportunity.

This chapter has emphasized the importance of low and flexible pricing as the key for establishing market value for products or services. But flexible pricing does not mean discrimination.

FLEXIBLE PRICING AND DISCRIMINATION

Rural parts of emerging third-world markets represent low incomes and simple and frugal living. However, these consumers do have needs and, although limited, some economic means. As stated earlier, it is important for a company to allow room for negotiations with flexible pricing, which may mean lower prices in some areas. But flexible prices should not be construed as price discrimination.

As long as variations in price are not outrageously different and as long as existing variations are not very noticeable because other products also experience price variations, the conditions are acceptable and do not create ill will on the part of consumers. The distribution system that is handling a company's products may be given some lower limits below which the sale is not likely to yield any profit. Furthermore, the system may be advised as to the latitude it can exercise in pricing a product. In other words, participants of the system know how much of a discount they can offer below the asking price of a product.

SUMMARY

Although price-perceived quality is often practiced in the West, in emerging markets of the third world, that is not the case. Value in poorer markets is associated with price, durability, and performance of a product. In such markets, penetration pricing is critical. A company needs to penetrate as far as it can. Because third-world markets are made up of high-context cultures that use negotiation and because money is a scarce resource, prices are somewhat flexible. This flexibility is attributed to negotiation skills and a willingness to negotiate.

Target markets often have soft currencies, and partners in these markets accumulate these currencies, which are not accepted elsewhere in the world. Before entering a market, a company needs to have an agreement between its home bank and the central bank of the country it is considering entering.

Countertrading or bartering is another possibility. In some cases, a product-for-product exchange can be easier for a company to undertake than trying to find a way to use the soft currency. Barter arrangements are attractive for small, flexible international businesses.

REFERENCES

Arnold, David J. and Quelch, John A. (1998). "New Strategies In Emerging Markets," *Sloan Management Review*, Fall, 7-20.

Samli, A. Coskun, and Hill, John S. (1998). *Marketing Globally: Planning and Practice*. Lincolnwood, Illinois: NTC Business Books.

11

Adjusting the Strategy to Poorer Markets

A company may have more difficulty adjusting its ongoing marketing strategy to poorer markets. If a firm is dealing with major world markets, then directly adjusting its marketing strategy for a targeted third-world market is a very difficult proposition. In fact, this is another reason why global giants do not deal with the forgotten majority. On the other hand, without trying to scale down its marketing strategies, a large company dealing only with emerging markets or a small company developing its marketing strategy directly for a third-world market has a better chance for success. Whirlpool, after identifying four target markets in China, scaled down its activities to two markets and has not shown a strong presence in China or in the Indian market, where it also made an attempt to show a presence. Migros, a grocery chain that concentrates almost exclusively on third-world markets, has shown a presence in these two markets for the past 50 years. Migros plans its marketing strategies based strictly on the prevailing socioeconomic environment in its various emerging markets.

DEVELOPING A GOOD STRATEGY

Strategy is a company's game plan to accomplish its goals in a target market and to establish a respectable competitive advantage. But a strategy designed for industrialized world markets and scaled down for third-world markets is not as promising a marketing strategy designed specifically for a third-world market.

Since a marketing strategy is a company's game plan to accomplish its marketing goals, the company must decide what its plan of action should be. What are the company's marketing goals? First, the company wants to establish a corporate name with several product possibilities. Second, the company wants to establish itself as a "friend" of the secondary and tertiary markets or as a "friend" of people with limited means.

Third, the company establishes a good product or service line. Fourth, the company communicates information about its product effectively as possible. Fifth, reaching as deeply and as far as it can, the company proceeds into its target markets. Sixth, the company generates consumer value and delivers it efficiently and effectively. Finally, and most importantly, the company must establish itself as a leader and be competitive in defending its market.

There are five general competitive strategies. Figure 11-1 presents the way each is applied. A company must decide on the strategy that is most appropriate for its purposes and work to implement it.

A frontal attack is what BMW and Mercedes Benz are doing. Meeting competitors head on is not one of the alternatives of a company considering third-world markets. First, there are no competitors to attack in these markets; second, a small- or medium size firm does not have the capability to launch a frontal attack.

Outflanking, which is locating competitors' weaknesses and attacking them, is not possible for the same reasons a frontal attack does not work. Outflanking is not an alternative a company can use.

Figure 11-1. General Competitive Strategies

Type	Technique
Frontal attack	Meeting competitors head on
Outflanking	Locating competitors' weaknesses and attacking them
Encirclement	Producing more types, sizes, colors, and styles of products at similar or lower prices
Bypass	Ignoring competitors' present markets and technologies and doing something completely different
Guerilla warfare	Using local dealers and distributors to attack certain products, product lines, or channels

Source: Samli and Hill (1998).

Encirclement is producing more types, sizes, colors, and styles of products at similar or lower prices. Third-world markets are not interested in large varieties. Only simplified and low-price products appeal to this market. Thus, encirclement is not a strategy option for a company.

The last two alternatives (bypass and guerilla warfare) are the most appropriate options for a company's strategic goals and preemptive attempts against competition.

Bypass means to ignore a competitor's present markets and technologies and do something completely different. Basically, this is the strategy a company uses. There are no competitors; but even if there were, they would not go after the same market the company is contemplating entering. Furthermore, a product designed for a modest, low-income market is different from competitors' products, if there were such products. Additionally, pricing, promotion, and distribution activities are different from those of competitors, if there were competitors.

In a company's target market or a partner's market, a bypass strategy is appealing. The situation becomes a little more complicated when a company wants to enter a third market along with a competitor. Whether a company can use the same bypass strategy in a third market becomes a critical question. All the conditions that are present in a partner's market are present in the third market a company is considering entering. If a company cannot implement bypass, it cannot enter another market.

Finally, guerilla warfare means a company uses local dealers and distributors to attack certain products, product lines, or channels. But a company will use local dealers and distributors since it cannot develop its own distribution system. However, a company does not use local dealers and distributors to attack certain products or certain competitors; the company uses local dealers and distributors to penetrate certain secondary markets or target markets in emerging countries.

Of the five general competitive strategies, a combination of bypass and guerilla warfare is particularly appropriate for a company. The company is interested in markets that have been ignored up to now and is entering these markets with product lines designed specifically for consumers. The company is using local dealers and distributors to reach deep into these markets.

GUERILLA WARFARE—A NATURAL GAME

Guerilla warfare is a natural activity for a company. However, the word *warfare* is a bit extreme. When necessary, a company can preempt competition or react to it. However, the strategic activity being pursued is not a warlike activity. Entering and penetrating a market in the absence of competition cannot be construed as a war. Guerilla activity is a more appropriate analogy. A company must use local dealers and distributors to enter and penetrate third-world market. As a part of its overall strategy, the company's distribution must be adequate to reach and penetrate the target market. Instead of using all of the existing local dealers and distributors, the company (or its partner) decides on which ones to work with. If there is no competition, a company should not try to exploit the market and take as much as it can give. In second- and third-tier markets, a company cannot survive if it tries to get as much as it can. A company must enter a market, stay in the market, and generate consumer value. For third-world markets, this is the winning formula a company needs to follow.

Figure 11-2. Guerilla Activity Components Evaluation

Questions	Feature Evaluation
How well is the dealer or distributor known?	A company must work with a seasoned dealer or distributor.
How good is the dealer or distributor for entry?	A company must enter a particular target market effectively.
How powerful is the dealer or distributor in penetrating the market?	A company must penetrate the market as deeply as possible.
Can the dealer or distributor focus on the products and provide the attention necessary?	A company needs a concentrated effort from the dealer or distributor in order to enter the market and succeed.
Can the dealer or distributor change orientation, if necessary, to accommodate unexpected changes in the market?	The dealer or distributor must be flexible enough to help a company to cope with changes in the market.
What level of loyalty can be expected from the dealer or distributor?	A company must expect loyalty from the dealer or distributor—that the dealer or distributor will not abandon the partnership.

If a company wants to implement a guerilla strategy, it must select dealers or distributors it believes should carry its product. Selecting a dealer or distributor for a product or product line is based on six questions which are listed in Figure 11-2.

GUERILLA POWER

In implementing guerilla activity, a company must be connected to the proper dealer or distributor. What are the key criteria a company uses to select the dealer or distributor that is going to carry out its guerilla activity?

The dealer or distributor must have a positive reputation. It must be experienced enough to make our guerilla activity successful. A dealer or distributor that is reasonably well known functions well.

Has the dealer or distributor entered the target market with new products before? A company cannot afford to enter a market ineffectively, which means it must enter quickly with a lot of publicity and visibility.

The dealer or distributor must already be in the market and penetrating the market. Then the dealer or distributor can help a company penetrate the market the way the company planned. A dealer or distributor that cannot penetrate a market is of no use to a company. A company must be able to enter and penetrate. One without the other is useless.

Entering a market successfully and penetrating it deeply are not good enough if a dealer or distributor does not pay enough attention to a company's products. A company must have the undivided attention of its dealer or distributor. Without having its products being pushed through the channel, a company does not have a very good chance of success.

A dealer or distributor with good intentions is a necessary but not a sufficient condition, but good intentions alone are not enough. A dealer or distributor must be able to cope quickly and effectively with unexpected changes in the market. In other words, a dealer or distributor must be flexible enough to cope with a volatile market.

Finally, a dealer or distributor must have enough staying power to continue a relationship. A company expects loyalty from this important coworker. For instance, if another similar opportunity presented itself to the dealer or distributor, the company must know that the dealer or distributor would not abandon the existing partnership. If a dealer or distributor were to move on, the company would be left to handle a difficult situation. If guerilla activity has been ongoing and consumers know about the company and its product, there may be an emerging inertia whereby consumers are getting used to buying the company's product from certain kiosks or street vendors. If this activity is disrupted, the company may have a difficult time reestablishing itself.

GUERILLA POWER
SUPPORTED BY PROPER STRATEGY

Guerilla power goes way beyond the individual attention of a dealer or distributor. A proper strategy involves the strength that a dealer or distributor needs to push a product. Before such a strategy can be put into effect, a company needs a certain type of approach. This approach must have at least three features: sensitivity, compassion, and proactivity.

In second-, third-, and fourth-tier world markets, sensitivity is needed not only for better results in the marketplace, but also for sheer survival. To develop an effective strategy, a company must be able to understand is customers' point of view— to feel how they feel, understand what they need, and realize how their quality of life can be improved by the product being marketed.

However, sensitivity without compassion is not enough. Compassion means providing customers with the greatest value for the least cost. A Japanese executive says of his firm and his employees that they don't wan to satisfy their customers; they want to delight their customers. A company cannot just pay lip service to compassion; the company must demonstrate compassion.

In markets where changes are sudden and far-reaching, a company must be proactive. A company must be proactive by detecting important changes in the world and responding to them quickly using sensitivity and compassion by protecting the well-being of customers. This approach generates more profit in the long run.

Once a company has incorporated this general approach, a guerilla approach will be more successful. Generating familiarity in the marketplace for a product is the first big step. Assuming a company has developed locally desirable products (for example, cereals with local flavors, ski accessories appealing to local tastes, or reconditioned office equipment designed for local needs), the products must be introduced primarily through human interaction and retail store promotion. But generating familiarity may be timed so communication efforts precede introduction of the product. Since consumers are more involved in trying or sampling products, a company must facilitate these activities. Distributors, dealers, retailers, or street vendors must be informed about the importance of carrying out presale and sale activities in the market. In these communication efforts, the company name, the product, the product's durability, its value-generating characteristics, and (above all) its price must be emphasized. A company can create an aura of excitement in a small community rather easily. The company's local partner can provide guidance in that regard.

SUMMARY

Although there are a number of general competitive strategies, only two are particularly applicable to a company marketing in a third-world country. These are bypass and guerilla warfare. Bypass means to do something completely different. A company uses this approach since it is the only player in the secondary market, there is no competition.

Guerilla warfare is not the same concept in secondary markets as it is in primary markets. In guerilla warfare, companies use local dealers or distributors to attack competitors; in secondary markets, there are no competitors. However a company does use local dealers or distributors; without them, the company cannot succeed. Local dealers or distributors implement the company's strategy to enter and penetrate the market deeply. Simultaneously, they enhance the company's efforts to communicate with the target market and generate consumer value.

The strategy that is planned and implemented developed for a particular market. This is the strength of small- and medium-size firms; they do not develop a "one-size-fits-all" strategy.

Instead, their small size and flexibility enables them to develop various strategies designed for poor but potentially profitable markets.

REFERENCES

Samli, A. Coskun and Hill, John S. (1998). *Marketing Globally*. Lincolnwood, Illinois: NTC Business Books.

12

An Independent Entity

At the risk of being redundant, a company's size and organizational structure must be adequate to support a strategy designed for a poor market. But a company's true strength stems from its entrepreneurial approach. Such an approach enables a company to do things and to enter markets that other companies do not. As stated earlier, the global giants do not think of entering small emerging markets of third-world countries. Entering such unique and small markets calls for an entrepreneurial attitude.

ENTREPRENEURIAL APPROACH

We do not have to be a small proprietorship to be entrepreneurial. By the same token, being a small company does not mean it is entrepreneurial. The spirit of entrepreneurship has at least three critical dimensions: creativity, leadership, and performance. Figure 12-1 illustrates some of the details of these dimensions.

Figure 12-1. Dimensions of Entrepreneurship

Creativity	Leadership	Performance
• New Opportunities	• Sharing Responsibilities	• Having Industry Skills
• Knowledge	• Keeping Associates Informed	• Having Technical Know-How
• Vision	• Having Hands-on Experience	• Being Knowledgeable about International Issues
• Goals	• Being Able to Prioritize	
• Self-efficiency	• Being Focused	

The first dimension, creativity, has multiple features. Searching new opportunities is a critical starting point. Entrepreneurs explore different opportunities regularly. They are capable of identifying opportunities and taking advantage of them. However, identifying opportunities is not sufficient; entrepreneurs must have vision. Without it, they cannot enter and explore new areas or try new ventures that may be risky. Market risk exists because entrepreneurs are entering unfamiliar markets. It is difficult to derive accurate estimates about intended target market. Thus, uncertainty and unfamiliarity make the entrepreneur's risk doubly difficult (Zacharakis 1997). Because the entrepreneur has vision, risk taking becomes natural. The same vision allows the entrepreneur to foresee new business possibilities, expansion opportunities, and so on.

The achievement-oriented entrepreneur can establish specific goals easily. Setting up goals and accomplishing them are characteristics of successful entrepreneurs.

Entrepreneurs are self-sufficient. They know the skills they need, and they acquire these skills. In other words, they rely on their own Initiative to recognize their shortcomings and then they work to overcome these deficiencies. Of course, they are not afraid to ask for help, and they are capable of evaluating the help they get.

The second dimension of entrepreneurship is leadership. Entrepreneurs cannot accomplish everything. They need other people. Therefore, they must establish a reasonable level of leadership to accomplish the goals they are pursuing.

ENTREPRENEURIAL LEADERSHIP

Since the objective is to enter secondary and tertiary markets of third-world countries, however big or small, a team must be composed of people with different skills. The first aspect of entrepreneurial leadership is sharing responsibilities. A good entrepreneur does not try to do everything himself or herself. A team must have the skills and knowledge necessary to achieve the goals of the overall strategic plan. Thus, entrepreneurship calls for making sure that the responsibilities are identified and allocated according to the skills and knowledge of the team.

The first aspect of sharing responsibilities means keeping associates informed. The entrepreneur has a vision. This vision is to be implemented. The implementation process begins and continues with keeping associates informed. In addition to understanding their role in the process, they need to understand how the process is progressing. This creates a feeling of togetherness and accomplishment.

Of course, the entrepreneur, in attempting to implement the vision, must be involved in the implementation. The, entrepreneur must have ongoing and hands-on involvement.

PERFORMANCE DIMENSION

As entrepreneurs acquire hands-on experience, they develop refined industry skills. Besides being able to identify emerging opportunities in certain industries, they must know how to take advantage of the circumstances.

Industry skills are necessary, but an entrepreneur needs more. An entrepreneur, in this day and age of globalization, must have technical know-how. The entrepreneur must be able to access new information and obtain new technical skills. The entrepreneur needs knowledge about international issues.

Successfully choosing certain secondary or tertiary markets in third-world countries is a result of being knowledgeable about international issues. But this knowledge needs to be supplemented by the ability to prioritize. An entrepreneur cannot take advantage of every opportunity. An entrepreneur must make a decision as to which opportunity to capitalize on.

Finally, the entrepreneur is highly focused. Once a decision is made to pursue a certain opportunity, the entrepreneur follows through on this decision, making it a reality.

Thus, an entrepreneurial company takes risks but also has a compelling desire to succeed in its chosen target market. The company must be able to articulate, differentiate, and prioritize its opportunities so it can choose the best one.

Entrepreneurship must also lead a company in the direction of establishing a synergistic relationship with a local partner. It is highly unlikely that a non-entrepreneurial partner can give a company the opportunity to establish the synergistic relationship needed for success. In many cases, entrepreneurs rely on agents to enter foreign markets, as discussed in Chapter 1. Nova Biomedical Company worked with an agent to enter the Iranian market. The agent helped negotiate with the government and with hospital administrators and received the necessary permits. Spyder Sports designs and produces ski accessories. The company used 11 export agents to enter 11 separate markets worldwide (Zacharakis 1997).

How a company finds entrepreneurs (agents, distributors, and manufacturers) to partner with and how a company motivates them are important questions. Put in more general terms, how can a company maintain its entrepreneurial characteristics and still manage an entrepreneurial alliance? Although Chapter 5 discussed some aspects of partnering, it is critical to examine a more refined version that deals with entrepreneurial management is discussed here. Figure 12-2 presents an entrepreneurial alliance management model. Here the emphasis is on a company maintaining its entrepre-

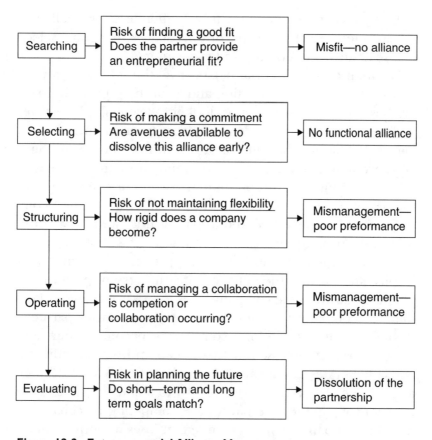

Figure 12-2. Entrepreneurial Alliance Management

Source: Adapted and revised from Das and Teng (1999).

neurial characteristics and creating a synergistic alliance with a partner who also is an entrepreneur.

ENTREPRENEURIAL ALLIANCE MANAGEMENT

If a company wants to enhance its entrepreneurial synergistic relationship and raise it to higher levels, the company must commit to that. To begin the alliance management process, a company must appreciate what it is doing and how much of a contribution a partner is going to make. The company must be willing to carry its operation to a higher level. The alliance management process has five distinct stages: searching, selecting, structuring, operating, and evaluating.

From an entrepreneurial perspective, the search for a partner must go beyond reputation and what the prospective partner has done. The search must look into leadership, creativity, and performance areas, as discussed earlier in this chapter. Figure 12-2 shows that there is a risk in not finding the right entrepreneurial local partner, resulting in a misfit alliance. When selecting an entrepreneurial partner, a company faces the risk of making a commitment with the wrong party. A company must be concerned about exit avenues and how to dissolve a relationship that is not working.

When a company finds an entrepreneurial partner and begins structuring the alliance, gearing it to perform to planned activities, the company faces the risk of losing its flexibility. A company must also be concerned about its partner's flexibility. Is it possible for a company to become rather rigid because, as was discussed in Chapters 5 and 6, it coordinates and collaborates with a partner? But there is also a risk of managing the collaboration. With regard to alliances, there is the question of whether the parties are competing or collaborating. If a company begins to compete, it loses its entrepreneurial synergism. The relationship should not result in one party winning and the other party losing, which is management. Poor management leads to poor performance.

Finally, a company must evaluate the performance of an entrepreneurial alliance. The company must plan future activities. Is the company going to continue as is, or is it going to expand? If the company plans to expand, will expansion be in another region of the same country or in a different neighboring country? Perhaps the most critical aspect of this evaluation stage is for the company to determine whether short-term and long-term goals are consistent. Otherwise, an entrepreneurial alliance may be in jeopardy. The company may not be capable of planning future activities, which would lead to dissolution of the partnership.

Trying to find a partner is easier than trying to find an entrepreneur as a partner. There are no specific tests or procedures, but the three dimensions mentioned in the first part of this chapter and presented in Figure 12-1 are the basic criteria. But how successful is a company likely to be in its evaluation of prospective partners for their entrepreneurial capabilities? A large number of corporate alliances in the industrialized world dissolve rather quickly. However, entrepreneurial alliances discussed previously could last and be successful much longer. Since the parties are not global giants, they can communicate and negotiate better. Although a company may not be able to function in, say, secondary markets of India or Turkey without having partners in those markets, together the company and its partners can become a real power and do well.

SUMMARY

This chapter reinforces a critical point of entrepreneurship. Unlike global giants, companies looking to sell to third-world markets are small, can move fast, can make quick decisions, and can be very efficient because they are entrepreneurial and because they have an entrepreneurial partner.

Entrepreneurship is an approach, not a size. A proprietorship does not need to be small to be entrepreneurial. A company must be creative, display leadership qualities, and perform in certain ways if it wants to consider itself entrepreneurial. But this is only half of the story. A company must also consider how to manage an entrepreneurial alliance. A company's partner also is an entrepreneur. A company must aim at having a synergistic operation without losing its independence. And a company doesn't want a partner to lose its independence and its entrepreneurial skills. Managing an entrepreneurial alliance requires five steps: search, select, structure, operate, and evaluate. If a company can perform these steps effectively, it is likely to have a successful well-managed alliance.

REFERENCES

Das, T. K. and Teng, Bing-Sheng (1999). "Managing Risks in Strategic Alliances," *The Academy of Management Executive*, November, 50-62.

Zacharakis, Andrew (1997). "Entrepreneurial Entry Into Foreign Markets: A Transaction Cost Perspective," *Entrepreneurship: Theory and Practice*, Spring, 23–40.

13

The Fairness Doctrine and a Sustainable Partnership

In large global corporations, fairness may not be a priority. These companies, when they enter into an alliance may try to take advantage of the situation and the partners, a concept called corporate imperialism. These corporations appeal only to rich markets and take advantage of their partners, which is why more that 34 percent of these alliances dissolve rather quickly.

In small synergistic and entrepreneurial alliances, such as the ones discussed previously, a company does not believe it can do without its partners and vice versa. Thus, the company develops a constructive relationship with a partner working for its success and betterment. The company appreciates its our partner and the value generated by its efforts. The company knows it cannot be successful without this synergistic alliance; therefore, the company must be fair in its assessment of itself with regard to its partner. Objectivity and fairness are necessary requirements in the establishment of an entrepreneurial alliance.

A PARTNER IS AN AXTENSION

Although alliances between companies from emerging markets and global companies appear to be total win-win situations, in reality, they are very difficult to manage. Why do alliances in emerging markets prove to be so difficult to manage? Management is difficult because global companies are insensitive, short-run oriented, and more materialistic. What they cannot accomplish can be successfully accomplished by a medium or small entrepreneurial firm that understands the usefulness of its partner. A company knows it is good, but also knows that without the alliance, it is nothing in the target market.

Adarkar, Adil, Waish, and Ernst (1997, p. 123) posit that "When an alliance is deemed necessary, both companies should assess at the outset how the partnership will evolve. Whether it is a marriage of equals that will endure, or something else. Achieving an equal balance in an emerging market is particularly challenging...."

This is where a small- or medium-size firm differs from a large global corporation. A partner is an extension of a company. Figure 13-1 illustrates the key tenets of this partnership. If a company cannot agree on the premises set forth here, it will not be able to get started. In short, what Figure 13-1 is saying is that without a good partner, a company cannot make it in the target market.

The eight tenets presented in Figure 13-1 are very important. Earlier chapters discussed what a company likes to see in its partners and what a partner likes to see in a company. But making this relationship an entrepreneurial and synergistic alliance takes a lot of work. A company should not lose sight of the important mechanics that will improve the relationship with its partner, creating a powerful alliance.

Figure 13-1. Mechanics of How to Treat a Partner

- A true partnership is created in which both parties benefit

- The company considers the partner as an equal (an extension of the company).

- Terms are set up front (based on a clear understanding).

- The parties represent each other equally, enjoying the same privileges.

- The parties develop a market strategy together.

- The parties do not move if they do not agree
  (all decisions are based on consensus).

- The parties trust each other and trust in what they are doing
  (they know their direction).

- The parties work together and together they succeed
  (success is based on joint effort).

Source: Adapted and revised from Patz (1996).

- A true partnership must be created in which both parties have is a lot at stake but also a lot to gain.
- The partner is considered an equal.
- The terms were not set up at the beginning of the alliance to be quickly changed. They were set up to ensure fairness.
- If the parties cannot represent each other equally, they have no business being together in an alliance.
- The parties must develop and implement a marketing strategy together Each party knows what the other needs to do.
- If the parties do not agree, they do not move. This is a basic concept if the parties want to work together.
- The parties trust each other and believe that what they are doing is right and that they will benefit from their efforts.
- The parties work together to generate consumer value, resulting in success.

A company's Western beginnings and its short-run orientation should not deter the progress that a synergistic and entrepreneurial alliance can accomplish. Dealing with second and third tiers of third-world markets, a company can look forward to the future, but must exercise a lot of patience. There is enough for both parties, which is the thinking and the direction that must be taken.

THERE IS ENOUGH FOR ALL

The mechanics of how to treat a partner presented in Figure 13-1 are important. If the parties generate market value, they generate profit, which is abundant in untapped third-world markets. But to capitalize on potential profits, a company must be in total agreement with its partner as to where they are headed.

The case of Wood Company, a producer of timber-processing equipment, is a good example. The company wanted to enter the Russian market by developing a joint venture with a producer and exporter of timber. The company was represented by a Russian expatriate who did not really understand the corporate culture in Russia. Wood Company sent this person to negotiate with a prospective partner. Wood Company developed a detailed and lengthy contract. The Russians wanted to form a relationship and came to an informal understanding before reviewing the contractual agreement. The Wood Company representative did not understand these wishes of the people with whom he was negotiating. The Russians wanted to emphasize marketing; Wood Company, finances. The project did not materialize (Snavely, Miassoedow, and McNeilly 1998).

Figure 13-2 presents six areas of agreement that are essential for parties to continue; in other words the parties continue their synergistic entrepreneurship successfully. Six questions need to be raised.

As the markets change in terms of size, demographics, or psychographics, a company must be in complete agreement with its partner. It would be very difficult to function if the parties saw the market differently from each other.

As the market changes, so does the profile of customers. Will the parties still be in agreement about that profile as it

Figure 13-2. Degree of Agreement

- Do the parties agree on the characteristics of the market?

- Do the parties agree on the profile of their customer?

- Do the parties agree on the proportion of local and international leadership that will carry them?

- Do the parties agree that they are learning together?

- Do the parties agree that yjey are going to expand?

- Do the parties agree on the direction of expansion?

changes? Without such an agreement, the parties have no place to go.

What proportion of the international leadership does a company exercise, and what proportion of leadership does a partner exercise? Do both parties agree with this proportionality?

Are the parties learning together as their experiences generate knowledge? If one of them is learning but the other is not, they cannot to continue successfully. The learning must be mutual, indicating growth and viability.

What about expansion? Is the partnership growing proportionately to the market? Should the parties expand beyond the existing market? These are critical questions that need to be answered if the parties want to survive and prosper.

Finally, if expansion is the goal, in what direction do the parties go? Which markets do they consider adequate for expansion, and what are the methods of such an expansion? Answers to the questions raised in Figure 13-2 would indicate a company's future tendencies.

FUTURISTIC ORIENTATION

A company planning to function in the second or third tier of third-world countries is futuristic. The company expects to enter the target market and be successful, although success will not come overnight. A company's entry in the market is followed by gradual but positive efforts to generate consumer value. In third-world markets, the present gives little, but the future promises a lot.

Having a futuristic orientation shows the difference between high-end niche players and low-end mass-market players. Hindustan Lever, a subsidiary of Unilever in India, partnered with a low-cost Indian detergent maker, Nirma, to become the largest detergent maker in the world in seven years. But this all happened because the company continued courting the tier two and tier three markets (Prahalad, Lieberthal, and Thurnau 1998). A company may not expect to become the largest in the world, but third-world markets have untouched potential, growing and waiting. A company can become a viable and profitable entrepreneur that makes a difference and generates consumer value. Remember that the second- and third-tier markets are composed of people who are beginning to learn that they have choices with regard to consumer goods. However meager their level of income, they will spend it to achieve a better quality of life. If a company and its partner work in that direction, they can accomplish a lot.

SUMMARY

This chapter makes a case against corporate imperialism. A company must not look down on its partner and not go after the first-tier markets only. A company must work with its partner synergistically and profitably. To treat its partner fairly and equitably, a company must consider the partner as an equal. Partners must establish their terms up front. They must represent each other equally. They must develop their market strategies jointly. If there is a disagreement, they should not move until it is resolved. Partners must trust each other and trust in what they are doing. Working together synergistic work will enable them to succeed. In addition, partners must see eye to eye as to where they are headed. They must be in full agreement about the characteristics of the market and see the customer in exactly the same way. They need to agree on the proportion of local and international leadership. They need to learn together. Finally, partners must agree whether to expand and what direction to take with regard to expansion.

REFERENCES

Adarkar, Ashwin, Adil, Asif, Waish, Paresh, and Ernest, David (1997). "Emerging Market Alliances: Must They Be Win-Lose?" *McKinsey Quarterly*, Autumn, 120–138.

Patz, Debby (1996). "10 Steps to a Successful International Partnership," *Folio*, Annual, 264–265.

Prahalad, C. K., Lieberthal, Kenneth and Thurnau, Arthur F. (1998). "The End of Corporate Imperialism", *Harvard Business Review*, July-August, 68–80.

Snavely, William B., Miassoedow, Serguei, and McNeilly, Kevin, (1998). "Cross-Cultural Peculiarities of the Russian Entrepreneur: Adapting to the New Russian," *Business Horizons*, March-April, 8–15.

14

Monitor, Monitor, Monitor

The size of a company has advantages and disadvantages. A small company has almost no bureaucracy, no stockholders to report to, and fewer organizational layers through which information and decisions must seep. Hence, a small company can move fast and decisively. However, a disadvantage of size is that a company does not have enough reserves or resources to fall back on when it is not doing well in the market. Thus, a small company cannot afford a wait-and-see attitude. On the other hand, since a small company is close to the market, it can get information quickly about its performance in the target market.

Because of limited resources and because a company is trying to accomplish a difficult task dealing with partners and unknown markets, a company must be proactive and open to information and reactions from the market. In second-, third-, and fourth-tier markets in emerging economies, if a company doesn't get a good start, it may not have a chance to make corrections because of the cultural emotionalism that prevails. For example say a consumer buys a new washer-dryer, the first in his or her lifetime. If the appliance does not work well, news will spread quickly in the market, creating negativism that may be almost impossible to overcome. A company must have very early indicators so a negative situation does not have a chance to set in. Financial criteria do not show problems soon enough. By the time a company discovered its product is not selling (and it is not making money), the damage is done. Early indicators allow a accompany to make quick adjustments. Changing the delivery system, making product parts available, or making similar key decisions can reverse the negative results early indicators may have shown.

EARLY INDICATORS

Although a business can develop its own unique early indicators, a few standard ones can be used effectively. Figure 14-1 presents four such early indicators.

In third-world markets, word-of-mouth communication is one way a company can detect the effectiveness of its performance early on. With a high-context society, human interaction is predominant. A company should not have difficulty becoming privy to such word-of-mouth communication, learning what the market is thinking about the product and about the company.

If demand for a product is high and dealers cannot keep the product in stock, the product is obviously a smash hit. The only thing a company must to worry about is that the product is not just a passing fancy. Therefore, the company must make sure it is not the newness and availability of the product, but its qualities and performance, that are causing the high demand.

Although they live in high-context cultures, many third-world consumers may not be forthcoming with complaints. (This may be due to earlier negative political experiences, or it may be the nature of the culture.) Therefore, a company should not expect a lot of formal complaints. However, informal complaints may be substantial. A company must know how to handle informal complaints; for example starting a counter-

Figure 14-1. Early Indicators

Indication	Implications
Word-of-mouth communication	This indicates a noticeable reaction to a product.
A substantial increase in demand	Consumers like the product and worry that the market might run out of it.
Many formal and informal complaints	There are many problems with the product.
Requests for parts and repair	Consumers are anxious to keep the product, but the product has design problems.

rumor that all problems will be taken care of if the consumer just gets in touch with the company or the dealer.

If a product is not performing well because of mechanical problems, a company will bet requests for parts and repairs. Consumers are not returning the product; they want to keep it, but they want it to perform up to expectations.

Each firm is capable of developing its own early indicators, which will prove to be more effective than the early indicators shown in Figure 14-1. These indicators can result in the company making quick adjustments, which is part of the control mechanism. Since bad news spreads much faster in high-context cultures, making quick adjustments is essential for a company's survival and success.

Without early indicators, a company would have a difficult time monitoring its efforts and performance. As was mentioned earlier, emotionalism is a characteristic third-world markets. Therefore if the market has a negative experience with a company's product, a company may not be able to remedy the situation. Thus, early indicators followed by quick remedial action are critical for a company's survival in its target market.

Early indicators must activate a control mechanism that is already in place. The procedures must lead to corrective actions or generate modifications in marketing plans, depending on the issues the company faces.

A CONTROL MECHANISM IS NECESSARY

Figure 14-2 presents a complete control system. Even no negative vibrations are coming from the market, a company must review its activities regularly and look for areas needing improvement.

A company's control mechanism must begin with self-evaluation. Does the company have the proper mind-set for success? Did the company make the right decisions, and is it continuing with those decisions? Is the company as enthusiastic today as it was when it started its marketing venture? These are far-reaching questions and must be answered affirmatively in order for a company to carry on.

If a company is still enthusiastic about its venture, the first thing the company must do is examine its product and service. Suitability of its product or service is a company's the most important consideration. Is the company generating enough consumer value to ensure a strong position in the target market? If the company is unsure about the answer to his question, it may decide to end its marketing venture before becoming too involved.

What about the company's entrepreneurial approach? Is the company still enjoying its entrepreneurship, and is the venture paying off? Can the company further benefit from this special feature that got it where it is? Can the company generate follow-up goods and services and expand in the direction originally planned? If a company is not as entrepreneurial as it thought it was or if its entrepreneurial spirit is fading away, the company may have difficulty continuing unless it changes the whole approach of is current activity, which may be impossible to do.

If we are in the wrong market, very little can be done except discontinue the operation. Did we identify our target market carefully? Are we quite confident about the characteristics of our target market? Did we profile our customers appropriately? These are very important questions. It may not be as dramatic as discontinuing the operation. Some modification of our perception of the market can bring us closer to generating more

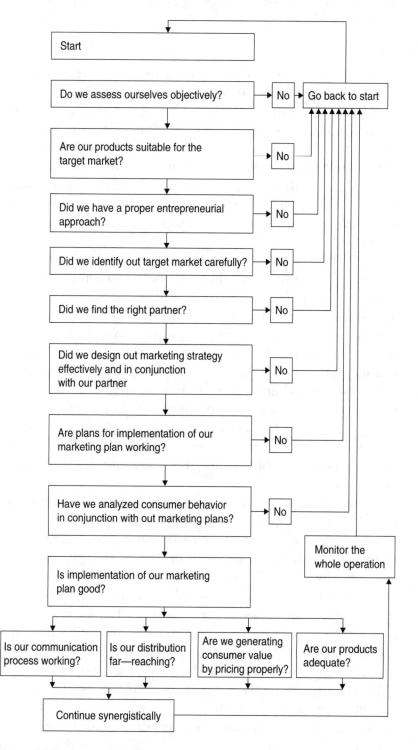

Figure 14-2. Control Mechanism

and better consumer value. An improvement here can be significant in terms of enhancing our market power.

One of the most important areas in a company's control mechanism is the evaluation of its partner. Did the company choose the right partner? A negative answer to this question brings the company back to the starting point. Not only must a company be objective in its assessment, it must also understand that choosing the wrong partner can result in the company's failure. If a company is doing well, it must give credit to its partner.

The answer to the question of whether a company designed its marketing strategy effectively is rather obvious. Either the company is doing well or it is not, and in the final analysis, the overall impact of the implementation of the strategy will surface as the company examines its performance. Here the company examines its own general approach in the target market and its partner's participation in the overall activity. The company's design and implementation of its strategy are two separate issues. A company must be able to assess and diagnose the strategy it is using. If, for instance, a company's strategy emphasizes reaching out to rural consumers in a region but the distribution system is not reaching these consumers, the company has a problem.

In the implementation of a marketing plan, consumer behavior becomes a critical issue. Is a company's marketing strategy consistent with consumer behavior? Furthermore, is the company's strategy implementation congruent with the consumer behavior prevalent in the target market? For instance, if a company has almost no personal communication in marketing a product in a high-context culture, it is creating a mismatch between the implementation of its marketing plan and consumer behavior. In a high-context culture, consumer interaction is a critical factor in market communications.

Evaluation of a marketing plan goes far beyond matching it to consumer behavior. Evaluation involves looking at the implementation of the plan from a perspective of communication, distribution, price and product. If a company is not communicating well, its product may become a best-kept secret. In a market economy, this lack of communication is not acceptable. Communication with the market must be a deliberate act. A company must know what the market is thinking. A company has a problem when what the company attempts to communicate is different from how the market perceives the communication. The sooner the company discovers this problem, the sooner it can rectify the situation.

Is a company distributing its products adequately? How far-reaching is the company's distribution system? Are products reaching customers? These are critical questions that a company must answer. A company 's distribution system must reach its consumers even though transportation may be a major economic issue in the market. Consumers may not be very mobile. Can a company partially address this problem by carrying the goods just a bit closer to the consumer?

A company's goal is to generate consumer value. As a result, the company makes a profit. Consumer value in emerging third-world markets is more than price. It is a three-pronged concept. Price combined with performance and further combined with quality generates consumer value. Properly pricing a product raises many questions. How much can customers pay? Is the price reasonable given customers' lifestyles and economic well-being? How well does the product perform? Do price and performance make a good value combination? Do consumers like what they perceive to be quality? Any suggestions from the customer about a product's price, performance, and quality can make a company's overall efforts to generate consumer value much easier.

Finally, the last question a company must consider is whether it has a good product. All other considerations become moot if the market does not perceive a product to be adequate. Evaluating the market's perception of a product can also lead a company to product ideas that can be developed in the future. Because of their limited economic means, consumers in third-world markets are focused on price, performance, quality, and product links.

Regardless of how big or small a business is, these monitoring details must be in place. A company cannot afford to say that only big businesses need such a monitoring system. Dealing with a sensitive market, a smaller firm must be cautious and very proactive in making necessary changes as quickly as possible. Proactive behavior in sensitive and changeable markets is critical. The control mechanism is a natural tool of such behavior. If a company expects to last a long time in the market, as was described earlier in the case of Migros, it must have a very agile and responsive control mechanism.

THE FUTURE BELONGS...

Out of a population of 1.1 billion in India, the "consuming class" is expected to reach 450 million by 2010. The new entrants to the middle class are not replications of the old middle class consumers. The newcomers are much less predictable and understandable. Their wants may not be well known, but their actions are easy to observe. They are buying two-wheelers and motorcars, washing machines, televisions, cell phones, air conditioners, and designer clothes. They are becoming more upwardly mobile and better educated (*The Week,* December 30, 2001). Similar activity can easily be observed in China, Indonesia, Brazil, Argentina, and Turkey. The point is that the more upwardly mobile the forgotten majority becomes, the greater the opportunities for entrepreneurial small businesses to cater to small but dynamic market segments. Monitoring, therefore, is not only looking at what a company is doing and how well it is performing in the market, monitoring also involves knowing what is happening elsewhere. The forgotten majority is slowly but surely becoming a profitable market for entrepreneurs. The future belongs to those proactive and entrepreneurial businesses that will capitalize on the first mover advantages. Being the first company to enter an up-to-now ignored or forgotten market is likely to generate much loyalty and profit. Monitoring is necessary to identify new market opportunities.

SUMMARY

A company cannot wait to find out it is performing poorly after reading the financial reports. By then it is too late. A company must have a series of early indicators of performance: word-of-mouth communication, a substantial increase in demand, many formal and informal complaints, and requests for parts and repair. Since each business is unique, each business should develop its own early indicators.

Beyond the early indicators, a company must deal with a control mechanism. The early indicators can lead a company to activate the control mechanism early on. The control mechanism begins with self-evaluation and moves in the direction of partner evaluation and market reevaluation. It proceeds further in the evaluation of the marketing strategy and then the implementation of this strategy. The marketing strategy and its implementation are evaluated in terms of how they fit with the characteristics of the target market. Finally, a company's evaluation of how well it communicates with the market, how well its distribution system is working, whether it is generating adequate consumer value, and, how good its products are provides the foundation for change, revision, and improvement. Such a control mechanism should be in place for any business in any market, regardless of size.

REFERENCES

The Week (2001). "The Giant Indian Middle Class," December 30, 14–47.

15

The Future Outlook

T his book has discussed the second wave of globalization that will bring the second-, third-, and fourth-tier
markets of the third world into the globalization
process. This development will benefit everyone involved and
will expand the sustainability of the current globalization
movement.

This book is about remembering the forgotten majority.
Many multi-nationals have not been anxious to enter third-
world markets preferring instead to enter the markets of the
industrialized world from the high end and becoming luxury
niche players mostly in the first tier. This is what is called corporate imperialism (Prahalad and Lieberthal 1998), which
leads in the direction of a worsening of the economic balance
of the world (Samli 2002).

If the second wave of globalization does not become a
reality, the gap between the haves and have-nots becomes so
large that the first wave of globalization will not remain sustainable. If the gap between the rich and the poor widens, everybody loses; if that gap narrows, everybody wins. But besides that,
corporate imperialism must change because much money can
be made in third-world markets. The giants of global markets

must change their attitudes, shift their resources, and develop a more innovative approach. Because it is almost impossible for large corporations to get into such a mind-set and make such adjustments, the best growth opportunities in the third-world markets are for entrepreneurial small- and medium-size companies. Small entrepreneurial firms can adjust to these market settings more easily than their large global counterparts. This is because they do not carry corporate baggage that restrains their actions and flexibility. The smaller entrepreneurial firms must ally themselves with partners in order to enter these third-world markets and to become successful.

Smaller companies are simpler organizations, more agile, more entrepreneurial, closer to markets, more sensitive to market needs, and capable of generating consumer value in third-world markets. These companies do not have traditions to undo or knowledge to unlearn. Hence, they are ideally suited for marketing opportunities in the third world. However, many of these smaller entrepreneurs do not perceive the existence or emergence of international opportunities until they are contacted by a local agency or a foreign customer. Even if they were cognizant of these opportunities, they often do not possess the initiative, the resources, and the necessary expertise to enter international markets (Zacharakis 1997).

Chapter 6 discussed home front alliances and target market alliances, which help an entrepreneurial firm get hooked up with international export support systems. Throughout this book, it has been reiterated that local cultures are different and, as such, they have different needs. Whereas the global giants are more geared to the "one-size-fits-all" approach to world markets, small entrepreneurial firms can cater to local needs by varying their products, services, and strategies, making money as they create consumer value.

But they cannot succeed these unless they have capable local partners. Finding a partner and working together is a challenge. Small Western entrepreneurs that hope to expand internationally need help. Countries and regions can provide help in the form of matchmaking; that is, offering facilities in their areas for the companies looking to expand there.

Similarly, entrepreneurial businesses must establish effective communication with prospective partners. This is not an easy task. International matchmakers must be genuinely interested in creating synergistic matches so all parties can benefit.

Attempting matchmaking and creating communication between prospective partners are critical factors but more is needed. International matchmaking organizations should also be in a position to referee conflicts and misunderstandings that may occur. Such organizations are not plentiful. Developing a class of international matchmakers is one of the most critical requirements of the ongoing globalization process.

Finally, international matchmaking organizations should be close enough to both parties to provide support in order to reinforce relationships. Such reinforcement may be necessary for the partners to become more synergistic. For example, if a company's products are not distributed in every store, available only in bazaars and kiosks, a matchmaker can bring the company and its partner together for a discussion about how to improve the situation. A competent and versatile international matchmaking group is needed.

Matchmakers, along with other outside agencies, must perform additional key functions to create consumer value and profit for all participants. These four functions, which are critical for remembering the forgotten majority, are identifying market opportunities, locating entrepreneurs, developing a support service system, and arranging for financial support.

OUTSIDE AGENCY FUNCTIONS

This book discussed opportunities in the markets where the forgotten majority lives. Identifying these opportunities and these markets is very important. Home-front alliances and target market alliances, which are composed of one or more agencies (See Chapter 1), must provide this opportunity.

The second function is related to finding entrepreneurs. A manufacturer of refrigerators from Florida or a food processing firm from Michigan may not be aware of third-world marketing opportunities, but they are entrepreneurial enough to initiate activity once they learn about them.

The third function is creating a support service system. What this concept implies is that a prospective international businessperson from the West is given many opportunities to enter the world of the forgotten majority. Part of this support system was presented in Chapters 1 and 10 in the discussion of homefront alliances and target market alliances. A number of services need to take place in addition to the function of the international matchmaker and other support activity discussed thus far. From coming up with product development ideas to making local deliveries to communicating with the target market, many detailed functions must be performed.

Finally, and perhaps above all, financial support must be provided, perhaps in the form of a global financial system, as illustrated in Figure 15-1. The local, regional, national, and international links of such a system must be put in place. A system should provide financial and political assurance in addition economic incentives. Along with local participation, this international financial system must be present and functional. It may be part of economic aid for development, which is a nonprofit activity, or it may be part of a financially profitable venture that is privately financed and adequately insured.

A small entrepreneur does need help, particularly until the business venture is working well and the company's presence in the target market is a reality. The end of corporate imperialism must come about as the result of companies dealing effectively with multiple cultures and entering markets from the lower end.

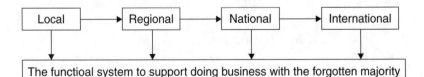

Figure 15-1. A Global Financial System

ONE WORLD MULTIPLE CULTURES

It has been estimated that there are about 3,000 languages in the world. This means that at least 3,000 different cultures exist in the world. Each culture has different values, different behavior patterns, and different needs. This fact alone sheds much doubt about the appropriateness of the "one-size-fits-all" philosophy of global corporate imperialists and provides a strong argument for catering to these cultural needs. Many of these cultures or markets are not rich, but they do have needs and they do have some means to buy products and services. Above all, these poorer markets with unsatisfied needs are the forgotten majority. They represent marketing potential during the coming decades. With a little outside help, small and medium entrepreneurial entities can be successful in these second-, third-, and fourth-tier markets of the third world. Entering and functioning in these markets means profit to those companies who create consumer value (Terpstra 2000).

The completion of a research agenda by entrepreneurs an the regional and national export agencies will reverse conditions in the forgotten parts of the world, making them important, profitable markets for entrepreneurs.

A RESEARCH AGENDA

Figure 15-2 puts forth five key areas that need to be cultivated for remembering the forgotten majority.

How to encourage more participants or more participation is the critical first question. What would make a Turkish textile development company open one plant in Iran and another plant in rural Brazil? If this question can be answered, more and better economic activity in these parts of the world can take place, enhancing the quality of life prevailing in these areas.

The second key research question is related to developing matchmakers. Developing entrepreneurial businesses in parts

Figure 15-2. A Research Agenda for Regional or National Agencies

Research Question	Impact
How is participation encouraged?	More and better activity to improve the quality of life in third-world countries
How are international matchmakers developed?	The starting point for remembering the forgotten majority
What specific functions should the support systems perform?	Expanding activities in the forgotten majority markets
Is there a way to develop special funding for doing business in third-world countries?	Developing the key tenet of the second wave of globalization
How is international entrepreneurship developed?	Sustaining globalization by remembering the forgotten majority

of the world where the forgotten majority resides is partially connected with the efforts of players who participate in home-front alliances and target market alliances. The establishment of support systems that start the entrepreneurial process rolling is a critical aspect of remembering the forgotten majority. Local communities and government authorities in third-world areas must encourage businesses to become more involved in these markets. Each community may have different ideas about how to generate matchmakers. Much research is needed before the communities can accomplish this task, which leads to the third key question.

What specific functions should the support systems perform? Is there a way to identify what support services the small entre-preneurial companies need so they can successfully participate in remembering the forgotten majority? If standardized lists of activities are formulated and used successfully, all parties can benefit.

The fourth research area in the agenda involves funding. As mentioned earlier, an international funding system that finances business with the forgotten majority is an important step in the right direction. The nature of this funding agency and how the funds are collected and used are critical areas that need to be investigated. One possibility may be a special bank that is supported by private and public funds. However, The International Monetary Fund (IMF), the World Bank, and representatives from third-world countries may have better ideas that can be put to use. The much-needed second wave of globalization will become a reality when this funding research becomes a reality.

Finally, even though the second wave of globalization is not in full swing, facilitating the development of an international entrepreneurial group is in order. Such a group is necessary in the development of third-world economies. This group will carry the important task of marketing to masses in third-world countries. Remembering the forgotten majority is the single most important task for international entrepreneurs. It may mean the end of corporate imperialism and a new beginning for a fair and sustainable globalization process that the world needs desperately. Above all, it will mean successful marketing opportunities for international entrepreneurs.

SUMMARY

The future outlook of international entrepreneurship that will play a key role in remembering the forgotten majority is questioned. This area of research must be taken seriously so the forgotten majority is remembered and so entrepreneurs can profit as they generate consumer value.

A basic research agenda must be seriously considered and expanded into plans for implementation. This agenda involves answering five questions: How is more participation encouraged in remembering the forgotten majority? How are international matchmakers developed? What specific functions should the support systems perform? Is there a way to develop special funding? How is international entrepreneurship developed? Answering these questions and remembering the forgotten majority is a challenge facing the twenty-first century.

REFERENCES

Prahalad, C. K., and Lieberthal, Kenneth (1998). "The End of Corporate Imperialism," *Harvard Business Review,* July-August, 68–80.

Samli, A. Coskun (2002). *In Search of a Fair, Sustainable Globalization.* Westport, Connecticut: Quorum Books.

Terpstra, Vern and Russow, Lloyd C. (2000). *International Dimensions of Marketing.* Cincinnati: South-Western College Publishing.

Zacharakis, Andrew (1997). "Entrepreneurial Entry Into Foreign Markets—A Transaction Cost Perspective," *Entrepreneurship: Theory and Practice,* Spring, 23–40.

POSTSCRIPT

Perhaps some of the ideas presented here should have been included in the last chapter. However, this Postscript was written after Chapter 15. But connecting the contents and the orientation of this book to the bigger picture is very important; hence the Postscript.

The aim of this book is to emphasize the fact that entering and functioning in the emerging markets of the world is profitable. But it is also a very important way of spreading globalization in a balanced and beneficial manner. World and regional authorities and other NGOs would be well advised to accelerate the process of Western entrepreneurial firms entering emerging third-world markets so globalization can reach out and benefit these markets. This bottom-up approach to globalization is not only profitable at the micro level, it is also necessary at the macro level. In fact, this approach is the future.

INTRODUCTION

Stiglitz (2002, p. 214) states, "Globalization today is not working for many of the world's poor. It is not working for the environment. It is not working for the stability of the global economy." He sets the tone of this all-important topic, GLOBALIZATION. Today, of the 100 largest economies in the world, 51 are corporations and only 49 are different nation states. The sales of General Motors and Ford are greater than the GDP of total sub-Saharan states in Africa. Wal-Mart has total sales higher than the revenues of most of the states of Eastern Europe. Today's globalization, unchecked, is likely to continue in the same direction (Hertz 2001).

At no other time in the history of humanity has there been as great an opportunity for globalization to stimulate the growth of third-world economies. Although not a recent phenomenon, globalization has been emerging at an accelerated pace. Current globalization is taking place as a result of four special flows: capital flow, information flow, technology flow, and know-how flow. In fact, these four flows, when used correctly, are key instruments for the development of third world countries.

In fact, through these four flows, globalization is creating miracles. The four tigers (Singapore, Hong Kong, South Korca, and Taiwan) would not have come into being without the four flows. Many other countries are also benefiting from globalization. But the current wave of globalization is not likely to receive a good grade.

Despite its capabilities to deliver economic development, globalization, as it stands, is resulting in a widening gap between the haves and have-nots in the world. Thus, even though globalization can be considered a major (and perhaps the only) vehicle for economic development of some third-world countries, this vehicle is not working well enough. Globalization must be used effectively and deliberately if it is to become the single most powerful means for economic development. Without proper economic development, discussion of quality of life (QOL) is an exercise in futility. The improvement of QOL in third-world countries is predicated by economic development. This Postscript presents an approach to making sure that globalization will reach out and benefit the poor. This section presents a need for a second wave of globalization that can benefit third-world countries before it is too late.

THE FLOWS AND REALITIES

The current wave, or the first wave, of globalization works primarily on the basis of four flows.

Capital flow has made it possible for foreign direct investments (FDIs) to come into being. Global giants such as Ford, General Electric, Nokia, and General Motors have been joint venturing, investing, and partnering, but in all cases relying on the capital flow to enhance their global presence.

Information flow through cyberspace developments has helped the expansion of international trade, research, and international communication. This flow of information enabled many firms to internationalize. It also stimulated consumer demand worldwide for more sophisticated and expensive products.

Technology flow is the most important aspect of globalization that can help third-world countries. While many less developed countries may not be able to develop technologies, they can successfully receive and utilize technology to best advantage. Through this technology transfer process, in many parts of the third world, pockets of competent suppliers have emerged. They have expanded their involvement in international trade.

Finally, know-how flow has made it possible for many companies in many countries to get the best and most competent managerial talent and advice. Top management teams and CEOs are more multinational than in the past. Despite these strong flows, globalization is still more of a liability than an asset.

These flows are generated and accelerated by four key developments that have been taking place during the past two decades or so: decentralization, deregulation, privatization, and cyberspace development.

Decentralization has allowed companies to make, to sell, and to buy products throughout the world. In particular, ex-communist countries have experienced the decentralization of large industries that were previously owned and run by the government.

Deregulation is the slow elimination of barriers to trade. Efforts of the World Trade Organization and other agencies, along with the changing political postures of the world, made it easier to trade.

Privatization has been a hang-up of many ex-communist countries who have seen most of their industries become privatized. Each private company decides for itself what to make, what to buy, and what to sell.

Cyberspace development is perhaps the most important of these four factors that generate and accelerate globalization. Through cyberspace, it is possible to communicate with the whole world and sell anything and everything, as shown in

Figure P-1. All of the developments illustrated in Figure P-1 make it easy for small entrepreneurial companies to enter emerging world markets. Those who take advantage of these opportunities have the "first mover advantage."

Figure P-2 illustrates the immediate and unchecked negative powers of globalization and the resulting difficulties. A discussion of the overall impact of globalization follows.

The way globalization is described in the literature tells the story. Friedman (2000) described globalization as "Darwinism on steroids." If such an impact goes unchecked, added to an already worsening gap between the rich and the poor throughout the world, the problem is exacerbated. This worsening process is accelerating at a dangerous rate. It has been estimated that about 1.2 billion of the world's population live on less than a dollar a day. Additionally, Friedman (2000), in his description of globalization, talks about the rules of the process in terms of "the winner takes all," implying the far-reaching negative power of globalization. Since only the winner takes all and since there is only one winner, the others lose big. This situation, unchecked and continuing, can stimulate class wars within countries and terrorism internationally, particularly in the third world.

The third column of Figure P-2 explores implications about quality of life. If emerging world markets can provide a better

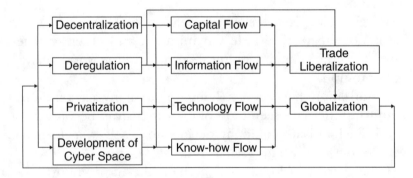

Figure P-1. The Globalization Process
Source: Samli (2002).

Figure P-2. Far-Reaching Impact of Globalization

The Impact	Outcome	QOL Implications
Big companies are gaining power.	Small companies are closing.	There are not enough opportunities for small entrepreneurs.
It creates global oligopolies.	It is catering to small rich markets, ignoring others.	There are only limited and selective benefits for the third world.
Information technology is used too much.	It is used negatively to overcome or defeat rather than build and gain.	Power is used negatively; winner takes all and leaves most behind.
It takes away jobs.	It is sending upscale jobs selectively to third-world countries.	Big domestic gaps result between the rich and the poor.
Newly created capitalist power is ignoring local political and cultural entities.	Local governments are losing power, and local cultures are threatened.	An identity crisis is creating confusion.
It destroys the environment for short-run profits.	No protective agencies or know-how exists in third-world countries.	There is a direct negative impact on the QOL of the unprotected.
Multinational corporations are flourishing.	Small local companies donot get a fair share of globalization benefits.	People are working hard but not receiving good compensation.
It benefits the already rich and advanced.	A lot of economic power ends up in the hands of a few.	Class wars in third-world countries results in hopelessness.
The gap between the rich and the poor widens.	If left alone, class wars at different levels will result.	The lack of economic power is causing negative QOL.

quality of life for their population, market opportunities for all will be greater. With regard to quality of life of the world's poor, globalization does not appear to be very helpful. From taking opportunities away from local entrepreneurs to challenging local cultures and authorities, globalization is creating adverse conditions for the world's majority.

A REPORT CARD

Despite its enormous benefits, globalization in its present form is failing to make the world a better place. This is due to four main gaps: the lack of a world order, a trickle-down orientation, the ignoring of possible benefits to stakeholders, concentration on bigger markets of the world, and no consideration of a bottom-up orientation of globalization.

The fact that there is no world order to direct, ease, and smooth the powerful and negative impacts of globalization necessitates the responsibility bestowed upon the powerful actors of globalization. These actors must see to it that participants (and even losers) receive some benefits in the process. This may mean more competition, but less greed. The winner may not take all, but only a large portion, leaving some of the proceeds to those who worked hard but did not win. In other words, globalization must move away from a win-lose to a win-win situation.

The trickle-down orientation, of course, is that global giants, as they wreak tremendous gains, are not concerned about weak local economies. However, as the global giants profit, there must be some small benefit for local economies. Unfortunately there is no global giant company or global authority to accommodate such a position.

Closely related to the trickle-down orientation is the fact that global giants, by concentrating only on major world markets, are ignoring, if not exploiting, third-world markets. This was described as corporate imperialism in earlier chapters of this book. These markets, in turn, are not gaining any ground in economic development. Somehow these countries are left behind with regard to obvious benefits of globalization that would contribute to their economic growth. Globalization flows must be taken to third-world countries, and a vitalization process must take place in these forgotten countries and markets. Remember that the majority of the world's population live in these countries where population increases more rapidly than the world's average.

Finally, closely related to the lack of concentration by global giants with regard to the forgotten markets of the world is the need for globalization to take a bottom-up approach. Getting more small businesses, developing an entrepreneurial class, and generating economic activity at the bottom level of third-world markets are necessary for small third-world markets to benefit from the four flows. But this is a major gap in the current pattern of globalization.

The discussion in this book leads to the need for another type of globalization, a type of globalization that remedies the four gaps articulated here. Thus, there is a desperate need for a *second wave of globalization.* When if the world economies develop on a bottom-up basis, the whole world benefits. Unlike the trickle-down activity that benefits only a few privileged companies and countries, a bottom-up orientation benefits the whole world. Therefore, a second wave of globalization is very desirable and profitable.

THE SECOND WAVE

The second wave discussed here relates to the nature of globalization, rather than to the time dimension of globalization. Some authors have referred to current globalization as the second or third wave. But their reference point is time rather than the nature of the current globalization process.

The nature of the proposed second wave of globalization is such that it must encompass at least a seven-step program, as discussed in Chapter 6. The most important point about this program is that it, too, is bottom-up and entrepreneurial. In other words, the second wave of globalization must begin with partnerships at the small business level. Western small and medium companies must be encouraged to enter the forgotten parts of the world, with a possibility of partnering. They need to understand that third-world markets combined are greater than Western and Northern European markets combined with North

American markets. Third-world markets are also estimated to grow much faster than the industrialized world markets. Thus, when small entrepreneurial Western firms partner with third-world companies, they are not doing this just to be good or helpful; they are doing it to partake in the expected growth of the dynamic emerging markets and to become profitable.

Finding partners, contacting them, and establishing mutually beneficial working relationships implies globalization through the four flows mentioned earlier. When these partnerships become viable, they provide economic benefit to the emerging third-world economies and accelerate their progress. Government officials and regional public organizations can accelerate this process by identifying and encouraging entrepreneurs from all parts of the world.

Once partnerships are formed, they can expand into local and regional networks. Such an extension of economic activity brings further economic benefits to all parties involved. In all cases, these networks are composed of small and medium entrepreneurial local businesses. By being part of the globalization process, these companies are not going to be wasted or squeezed out.

A network in one region can easily establish contacts with networks from other regions. These networks then can develop larger trading blocs that, in turn, trade with one another. Here the emphasis is on the less developed markets transferring technology and benefiting local economies as well. Another important point is that these trading blocs produce local economic wealth and consumer value simultaneously; they are close to local markets and their well-being is intimately connected to their ability to generate consumer value.

In an effort to jump-start the second wave of globalization, there must be local plans and international support organizations. Since the current globalization process is not sustainable and it requires the emergence of a second wave, something can be done about the whole picture. Unfortunately, no one acknowledges the need for such a position. The development and functioning of a second wave will be sustainable if it is given a head start. Such an activity would necessitate not a G-7 meeting, but a G-191 meeting. In other words, all of the world's countries must be involved in the development and functioning of the second wave. This second wave will enhance sustainability of the first wave, but will go substantially beyond that by expanding the outreach of globalization and by trying to make the whole world a beneficiary of globalization.

CONCLUSIONS

Globalization, in its current form, is being created by capital flow, information flow, technology flow, and know-how flow. Although globalization is an extremely powerful tool that can be used in a positive way to improve all of the economies throughout the world, as it stands, it is creating more difficulties worldwide. It simply cannot be sustained. The current globalization process is a trickle-down activity, there is no world order to control it, it does not consider the benefits of all stakeholders, it emphasizes only the rich world markets, and it does not take into consideration the well-being of those less fortunate. Thus, its contribution to the world's overall well-being is questionable. But the conditions are ripe for small entrepreneurs to take advantage of the opportunities in emerging world markets.

The proposed second wave of globalization is the opposite of the current one. It is based on a bottom-up, entrepreneurial, small business, and partnership approach. Partnerships expand into networks; networks, into blocs. Such an orientation does not leave many participants behind. It is sustainable and supports the current globalization process. Figure P-3 presents the key points presented in the Postscript. If the benefits of globalization are not far-reaching and emerging nations cannot receive some of the benefits, there will be many negative repercussions to globalization. Hence, it will be very difficult to sustain.

Figure P-3. A General Outlook

Globalization unchecked will cause:
- Class warfare domestically.
- Terrorism internationally.

Friedman's definition: Globalization is Darwinism on steroids.

Needed bottom-up, not top-down (or trickle-down), globalization.

Small and medium entrepreneurial businesses partnering with others in different markets is the solution.

Special emphasis must be put on emerging world markets rather than just the developed and industrialized elite markets.

Small entrepreneurial partnership must be established.

Partnerships become networks and networks becoming trading blocs.

Conditions are ripe for companies to enter and participate in markets where the action is expected to take place in a decade or less.

REFERENCES

Business Week (February 3, 2003). "Is Your Job Next?" 50–60.

Friedman, Thomas L. (2000). *The Lexus and the Olive Tree.* New York: Anchor Books.

Hertz, Noreena (2001). *The Silent Take Over.* New York: The Free Press.

Samli, A. Coskun (2002). *In Search of an Equitable and Sustainable Globalization.* Westport, Connecticut: Quorum Books.

Stiglitz, Joseph E. (2002). *Globalization and Its Discontents.* New York: W. W. Norton & Company.

INDEX

identifying, 31–34
multiple, 161
Currency, 116–117, 119
Customer profiles, 142, 150
Cyberspace, 1, 166, 167

D

Daewoo, strategic alliance with
General Motors, 67
Dangerous procedures, technol-
ogy transfer, 63
Dant, , xix
Dealers/distributors, guerilla
power, 125–126
Decentralization, 1, 167
Dell, 15
Demand, third world, 3–4
Demographics, 142
Demonstration teams, 109
Department of Commerce, 10
Department stores, 95
Deregulation, 1, 167
Direct distribution, 91, 96
indirect distribution *versus*,
91–93
Direct marketing channels, 91
Discrimination, flexible pricing,
118–119
Distribution channels
high-context cultures, 90–91
third-world countries, 89
Distribution of products, 80
Distribution systems
alternative, 94–96, 97
assessment, 155
evaluation, 153
performance, 92, 93
Durability, xxiii, 3, 86, 113, 119

E

Early indicators, 148–149, 155
Eastern Europe, 165

Economic features of products,
xviii, xxiv-xxv
Economic viability, 54
Economies of scale, penetration
pricing, 114
Elderly citizens
emotional messaging, 39
individualistic *versus* collectivis-
tic societies, 35
Emerging markets, alliances, 140
Emerson, globalization, 68
Emotionalism
reputation building, 105
role of early indicators, 149
Encirclement, 123
Energy technologies, 12
Entrepreneurial alliances, 134,
141
fairness and objectivity, 139
management, 134, 135–137
Entrepreneurial approach,
131–133, 150
Entrepreneurial firms, interna-
tional export support systems,
158
Entrepreneurial leadership, 133
Entrepreneurs, locating, 159
Entrepreneurship, dimensions,
132
Entry specific goals, convenience
alliances, 68
Entry strategies, 49
Environmental technologies, 12
Ernst, David, 140
Ethnocentric firms, 56
European cultures, Asian cul-
tures compared with, 30–31,
40
European Union market, size of,
xix
Evaluating step, alliance manage-
ment process, 136, 137
Exit avenues, entrepreneurial
partners, 136